Matthew M. Vriends, Ph.D.

Hedgehogs

How to Take Care of Them and Understand Them

With 43 Color Photographs;
Illustrations by Kees Vriends

BARRON'S

Photo credits
Barbara Aguello: pages 29, 88; Donald Franz: inside front cover, pages 5, 12, 13, 16, 17, 28, 48, 81, 84; D.J. Hamer, Jr.: pages 57, 60; Pat Storer: front cover, pages 8, 9, 20, 21, 24, 25, 32, 33, 36, 37, 40, 41, 45, 68, 69, 73, 76, 77, inside back cover, back cover.

About the Authors
Matthew M. Vriends is a Dutch-born biologist/ornithologist who holds a number of advanced degrees, including a PhD in zoology. Dr. Vriends has written over 100 books in three languages on birds and other small animals. He has traveled extensively in North and South America, the United States, Africa, Australia, and Europe to observe and study birds and mammals in their natural environment. Dr. Vriends is the author or advisory editor of many of Barron's pet books.

Pat Storer and her husband have been breeding and showing animals for more than 33 years and training them for over 40. Pat has been an officer and board member for various animal breed clubs and show chairman for several major animal events. She is a Licensed Chief Tester for the American Temperament Test Society and has developed a temperament and aptitude test for young puppies. She has written two books about hedgehogs and is the author of *Miniature Pigs* (Barron's).

The chapter "Raising Your Own Hedgehogs" by Pat Storer © 1994 County Storer Enterprises

All inquiries should be addressed to:
Barron's Educational Series, Inc.
250 Wireless Boulevard
Hauppauge, NY 11788

International Standard Book No. 0-8120-1141-4

Library of Congress Catalog Card No. 94-39684

Library of Congress Cataloging-in-Publication Data
Vriends, Matthew M., 1937–
    Hedgehogs : how to take care
of them and understand them . Matthew M.
Vriends ; illustrations by Kees Vriends.
        p.   cm.
    Includes bibliographical references
(p.   and index.)
    ISBN 0-8120-1141-4
    1. Hedgehogs as pets.   I. Title.
SF459.H43V75   1995
636'.933—dc20   94-39684
                                                CIP

Printed in Hong Kong
5678   9955   987654321

Contents

The "domestication" of hedgehogs is comparatively recent. Nevertheless, with proper care and management, these charming animals quickly become tame and affectionate pets.

Preface

Do you remember Mrs. Tiggy-Winkle, the hedgehog washerwoman from the charming tales of Beatrix Potter? Or the hedgehogs that were used as croquet balls in Lewis Carroll's *Alice in Wonderland*? Such delightful stories have entertained children for generations.

European animal lovers need not be charmed only by these famous fictional hedgehogs. They may also find the real thing—the European hedgehog, genus *Erinaceus*, in their own backyards!

There are no hedgehogs native to North America, though sometimes the porcupine is erroneously called a hedgehog. In recent years, however, a few enterprising fanciers have been breeding another species, the African pygmy hedgehog. This little animal is just 6 inches (15 cm) long from snout to tail, weighs just 1 pound (0.45 kg), and has been acclaimed as the perfect pet for apartment dwellers (it will do just fine in a backyard too!). It is a fact that these highly interesting and generally docile animals are rapidly gaining popularity among pet fanciers.

Originating in the African savanna, the African pygmy hedgehog has a special "pet-status" in Europe, when one considers that in most European countries it is illegal to keep the native European hedgehog as a pet. The native species is not neglected, however. Animal lovers feed the wild hedgehogs, especially in fall, to help them build up their body weight for the difficult period of winter hibernation. In certain regions a dish of minced meat or mealworms, placed outside the back door, will result in regular hedgehog visits, perhaps including a mother with a whole litter of babies! Sick hedgehogs are also cared for when the occasion arises. Indeed, it may prove difficult for some animal lovers to release their patients back into the wild when they realize how tame and trusting the creatures have become, almost as though they are offering thanks for the care that has been lavished upon them.

Although many fanciers are at first unaware of it, the African pygmy hedgehog is intelligent as well as cute, a fact that will reveal itself if the animal is given optimum and loving care.

It is important to point out here that these animals are not only suitable for adult fanciers. "Tiggy-Winkles" are also ideal pets for children to love and care for. It is not surprising that these animals are winning ever increasing numbers of friends year after year.

The purpose of this book is to provide all you need to know to properly care for the African pygmy hedgehog. It includes information on all aspects of housing, feeding, sickness, and, especially, behavior, both in the wild and in captivity. Other hedgehog species are also noted, and the reader will thus gain a complete picture of these interesting animals.

I have had the opportunity, over several decades, to care for many European and African pygmy hedgehogs as well as various other species. I have studied hedgehogs in the wild, and was involved in hedgehog research along with other experts in Europe as early as 1975. Since that

time I have usually had one or two African pygmy hedgehogs in my home. This book, therefore, has been authored not only by a scientist but, first and foremost, by an admitted and proud hedgehog fancier. Because I have both a scholarly and a personal interest in these charming animals, I welcome constructive criticism regarding the text and suggestions on further improving hedgehog husbandry. That way new information can be worked into any future editions of the book to provide the best possible guide to the care of these deserving animals.

It is important to be aware that the responsibility for adequate care of our pets rests with us. When an animal is taken into our home, it immediately becomes one of the family, and is thus entitled to all of the necessary and appropriate rights.

The author wishes to thank Fredric L. Frye, D.V.M., and the Dutch hedgehog expert Mrs. A. van de Werf for reading the text and offering useful suggestions. Thanks also to the staff of Barron's, especially Grace Freedson, managing editor, and Don Reis, senior editor, for their support and expertise. Last, but not least, I am indebted to naturalist and writer John Coborn, who, in many ways, significantly lightened my load.

Matthew M. Vriends, Ph.D.
Fall, 1994

For Tanya, Kimy, and Eddie.
Soyons fidèles à nos faiblesses.

Meet the Hedgehog

Order Insectivora

The group of mammals known as *insectivores* comprises a widespread and diverse group of animals. Most are small in stature, and share general basic features, but each group has its own special characteristics, designed for the particular way of life it follows. Insectivores comprise the most ancient order of placental mammals—i.e., those whose unborn young are nourished through a placenta, and indeed this nutritive organ is of a simpler form than that found in most other placentals.

Studies have shown that the ancestors of today's insectivores lived around 100 million years ago. Indeed, many of them shared the world with the dinosaurs! Today, insectivores are found in most parts of the world, from Australia to Asia, and on to Europe and Africa. They occupy a wide variety of ecological niches. Among the insectivores there are adept climbers, master swimmers, and others that have evolved special burrowing talents. Some island dwelling insectivores, such as those in Australia, New Zealand, and the oceanic islands, have become particularly specialized.

Anatomy of Insectivores

Most, but not all insectivores possess five toes on each foot. They have sharply pointed snouts and typically small eyes. All possess a collarbone (clavicle). They have up to 44 teeth in their jaws—a maximum for placental mammals. The teeth are usually crowned with sharp, pointed cusps.

The brain is relatively primitive, but this does not mean that the animals are particularly "stupid." The olfactory (smelling) and auditory (hearing) senses of all insectivores are highly developed, making them adept hunters and foragers. In hedgehogs the sight is reasonably well developed, but this is not so for all insectivores. Most moles, for example, have vestigial eyes. And you will see (page 58) that hedgehogs, for example, perform reasonably well in simple intelligence tests.

The Diet of Insectivores

As the name implies, insectivores feed mainly on insects, but they also prey on slugs and snails, spiders, young small mammals (rodents, for example), small reptiles, nestling ground birds, and any carrion they may find on their travels!

Being enormously active, and requiring vast amounts of energy, insectivores often consume their own weight in food every day. As many species are unable to find sufficient sustenance in the colder winters, they must hibernate, using the energy they had stored as fat during the bountiful summer.

Family Erinaceidae: The Hedgehogs

Hedgehogs occur throughout Africa and Eurasia, except in the most northerly zones. There are about six genera and some fifteen species, depending on which taxonomical authority you choose to follow. They occur in a variety of habitats from forest to desert.

Anatomy of Hedgehogs

Body and limbs: All species of hedgehogs have sharp, narrow snouts, small eyes, and short limbs, and are covered on the back and sides with barbless spines. The face, limbs, tail, and underside are furnished with "normal" mammalian hair. The two lower bones of the hind limb (tibia and fibula) are united. Most hedgehogs possess five digits on each of their feet, though some *Erinaceus* species have only four digits on the rear feet. There are five pads on the front feet and six (one of which is not readily apparent) on the hind feet. Hedgehogs have a *plantigrade* gait, meaning that they walk on the entire soles of the feet rather than the toes alone, and they leave a distinct track.

Teeth: Hedgehogs possess 36 to 44 teeth, the first incisors being notably larger than the rest.

Sexual characteristics: The male possesses a relatively large penis, which is hidden in a sheath that is outwardly directed and partially pendulous from the abdomen. In the female there is a very little space between the urogenital opening and the anus. There are two to five pairs of mammae.

Behavior of Hedgehogs

The Burrow

Hedgehogs are largely nocturnal, hiding during the day under fallen logs, among tree roots, in leaf litter, among rocks, or in burrows. They prefer a dry shelter, and may sleep either stretched out or curled up in a typical ball.

The European hedgehog (*Erinaceus europaeus*) usually occurs in wooded areas, but may sometimes be found in the mountains at surprisingly high altitudes. It is rarely seen in wetlands or on poor ground, such as coniferous woodlands, but often lives in suitable habitats close to human dwellings, such as parks and gardens.

An African pygmy hedgehog making eye-to-eye contact with an Atlas beetle.

Here it can construct its burrow and find a plentiful supply of food.

Types of Burrows: The hedgehogs of the genera *Hemiechinus* and *Paraechinus* in the Rajasthan Desert of India burrow into the ground with their forelimbs, throwing the earth behind them with lateral strokes. Once a sufficient quantity of earth has accumulated behind the animal, it uses its hind limbs to kick it rapidly out of the burrow.

Most of the European hedgehog burrows I've found in Holland and England were concealed by a thick layer of leaf litter and were usually situated under a hedge or a thick shrub. Sitting quietly and observing a burrow as night approaches, one will see first the sharp, quivering, inquisitive snout emerging from the leaves, followed, if the coast is clear, by the rest of the prickly body. I have been able to ascertain that hedgehogs always enter and leave the nest head first, meaning of course, that it must turn around while in the burrow.

Moving slowly and peacefully, these young hedgehogs are getting to know each other.

Foraging

When leaving a burrow at dusk, the hedgehog is always extremely hungry, and goes off hurriedly and noisily in search of prey. It has its own well-defined routes, and knows every nook and cranny of its territory, which it will have patrolled since its youth.

Juvenile Behavior

When a young hedgehog first leaves the maternal nest it gets to know its new surroundings in two different ways. First, the mother hedgehog takes it out in search of food. One sometimes sees a mother with a whole procession of little hedgehogs in tow. But the individual juveniles soon want to go out on their own.

At first they stay close to the nest and orientate themselves in the immediate area. With noses snuffling close to the ground, they inspect the area around the nursery. The next night they do the same, moving a little further away as they loudly snuffle about. Each consecutive night, their area of inspection becomes greater until, one night, they do not return to the nest.

They have become independent!

This form of behavior is found among many mammals. The first exploratory ventures influence the basics of future daily life. Little by little, the animal's knowledge grows, until it has a sound knowledge of its territory. Then it is able to spend more time in its direct living requirements, such as foraging for food, finding a good, safe, sleeping site, organizing good escape routes, and so on.

Hibernation and Aestivation

It is a well-known fact that European hedgehogs hibernate in the winter. This behavior has been thoroughly researched, but there has been little or no study of the aestivation (summer sleep) of the African pygmy or white-bellied (*E. albiventris*) hedgehog, or into the hibernation in the southern winter (May to August) of the South African hedgehog (*E. frontalis*). The white-bellied hedgehog can go into aestivation during the dry season, living from its fat reserves.

E. frontalis does not always need to hibernate, but can become quite sluggish during colder periods. Research into the subject of hibernation reveals more questions than answers, but it seems clear that all hedgehog species hibernate in one form or another. One must not forget that, for such research, the animals have to be taken out of their natural habitat and must function under controlled, experimental conditions. This is clearly far from ideal when one is concerned with physiological experiments, but at least some facts have become known about hibernating hedgehogs.

A hedgehog goes into hibernation (or aestivation) when little or no food is available. The fact that the white-bellied hedgehog goes into aestivation during hot and dry weather indicates that the local temperature has little or nothing to do with it. The long sleep is possible due to a dramatic reduction in the metabolic rate. This is not a continuous state; the animal wakes periodically.

The normal average body temperature of the European hedgehog is 95.5°F (35.5°C); The respiratory rate is 58 breaths per minute; the pulse is 265 beats per minute. During hibernation, the temperature falls to 42.8–50.5°F (6–10.5°C), the respiratory rate to 13 breaths per minute, and the pulse to 62 beats per minute.

During hibernation, a hedgehog has few defensive mechanisms. The animal remains sensitive to sound and touch in the area of the head, but it is so sluggish that it cannot respond adequately to attack. Blood clotting factors, as well as blood sugar, are lowered during hibernation. The death rate from wounds is high.

Spines and Defensive Behavior

When the hedgehog is foraging, the spines are laid back in the direction of the tail. When danger threatens, or when sudden sharp noises are heard, the animal rolls itself into a ball so that the head and limbs are hidden under the body. At such times, the spines, which are basically hollow, horny hairs, stand out. The hedgehog forms its ball by contracting the longitudinal muscles on either side of the body; it works like a sort of "drawstring."

When contentedly foraging with their typical waddling gait, hedgehogs emit continual grunting and snuffling noises. But when they are really anxious or threatened, hedgehogs let out a kind of noise similar to the hissing of a snake. When truly distressed, they can emit a loud scream.

The newly born young of the sub-species of the long- or big-eared hedgehog (*Hemiechinus auritus collaris*), have 2 millimeter-long spines that grow to .3 inches (8mm) in five hours. The length of the spine in adults averages 1.2 inches (30 mm). In the European hedgehog, the newly born young have soft spines that harden up in about three weeks.

In this connection, it is interesting to note the question posed by Dr. Maurice Burton, the well-known English zoologist: "Were hedgehogs once exclusively

A distressed hedgehog will erect its spines; a frightened hedgehog will roll itself into a ball.

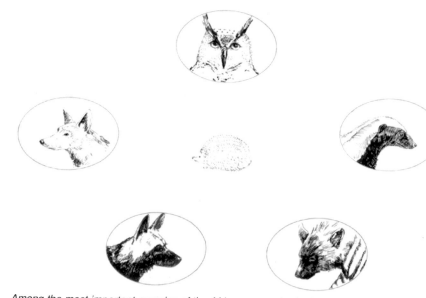

Among the most important enemies of the African pygmy hedgehog are (clockwise from the top) the great eagle owl, the honey badger, the striped hyena, the wild dog, and the jackal.

desert dwellers?" The question arose when he had studied cacti in the desert—plants that have developed spines in place of leaves, so that the evaporative surfaces are reduced to a minimum and moisture is thus conserved. There are indeed some desert dwelling hedgehogs that have "cactus-like" spines, but these are all nocturnal animals and would be exposed to the sun for longer periods only sporadically.

Although hedgehogs have numerous natural enemies (see page 66) the spines are generally an adequate means of defense. In most countries where hedgehogs occur, their chief enemy is not natural predators but vehicular traffic. The animals do not know that instinctively rolling into a spiny ball will not protect it against a lumbering truck or automobile! To make things worse, hedgehogs and their prey animals seek out the pleasantly warm surfaces of roads at night!

Breeding

Most hedgehog species bear litters of one to seven young, once or twice per year.

Hedgehogs as Pets

Lucky Europeans may be visited by wild hedgehogs in their own backyards. Many people help these animals through the more difficult periods by feeding them. The African species are also treated with kindness by people. This has been so for a long time, according to Egyptian hieroglyphic records, and Phoenician statues of hedgehogs are known.

The broad popularity of hedgehogs as "pets" has only developed comparatively recently. With adequate care and management, these charming, docile little animals soon become tame and affectionate (see the chapter, "Understanding Hedgehogs"). However, only the African pygmy hedgehog can be legally kept in most European countries. Other species are legally protected.

The African pygmy hedgehog phenomenon has a short history. In the mid-1980s these animals were imported for display in zoos. Raising them became rather popular, and the pet potential became obvious.

In 1993, "Hazel the Hedgehog" turned up in an American comic strip, and in that same year commercial hedgehog food became available for the first time. At about the same time, "Sonic the Hedgehog" began to appear in the cartoon that bears his name.

In general, African pygmy hedgehogs can no longer be imported, so the majority of available animals are bred in captivity. Rod Frechette, vice president of the North American Hedgehog Association (NAHA), see page 84), estimates that there are approximately 2,000 quality breeding animals in the United States.

This charming African pygmy hedgehog is asking for attention by standing upright and leaning against its person's leg.

Selection

Considerations Before Acquisition

Hedgehogs are clean and affectionate animals. With proper care and management, they can become excellent house pets. They are neat by nature, and clean themselves frequently.

Never obtain hedgehogs on impulse. Before acquiring any animal, give careful consideration to the possible consequences. Do you, for example, have sufficient time and patience to give the animal the care it deserves? Caring for any animal is a serious responsibility. If you have the slightest doubt about your ability to cope with hedgehogs, start with a single animal. Then you will be able to assess the amount of time and patience required for keeping several.

You must be sure, before the animal is purchased, that you have the time needed to properly take care of the animal. If this is not possible, you must make the decision that hedgehogs are not for you.

Since the introduction of the "bite-sized" hedgehog pellet in 1993, feeding your animals is no longer a tough job. But you need always keep in mind that commercial food alone is not enough!

A particularly time consuming, but necessary, task is the thorough cleaning of the cage every other day. Clean bedding must be available all the time. With inadequate care and feeding, a hedgehog loses condition and experiences stress. Disease quickly sets in, and can sometimes be incurable or fatal.

So, before getting started with this fascinating hobby, take heed of the old proverb, and look before you leap!

Do not yield to a hedgehog's obvious charm unless you are prepared to offer it loving care for eight to ten years.

The African pygmy hedgehog is an animal that requires loving care. You should not keep such an animal because you "want to own a hedgehog," but because you are prepared to care for it to the extent that it can live without stress and in good health for the length of its natural life (eight to ten years). You must, therefore:

• Have the time, patience, and, especially, the money to be able to adequately feed the animal, and to clean and disinfect its accommodations.

• Be able to make or buy a suitable cage for the hedgehog, and to keep it at a suitable temperature. A heat lamp and thermometer are required. And there must be an adequate sleeping box in the cage.

• Be prepared to accept the expense of veterinary care and treatment should your hedgehog get sick, or plagued with parasites.

• Ensure that, during its daily walk in the house, your hedgehog is not left jammed under furniture or caught in a self-closing door (to mention just two possibilities). At the same time, you and your family or guests must always watch out for the animal to avoid stepping on it accidentally.

• Be prepared to study this book, so that you get to know the importance of proper care and management, and become a member of the North American Hedgehog Association (NAHA) (see page 84).

A friendly hedgehog will keep its spines flat when being held by a trusted person.

13

Important: Always be present when young children are handling or playing with the hedgehog to ensure that no one is hurt. Children must be trained to respect the animal and learn the correct way to handle it.

Purchasing a Hedgehog

According to Rod Frechette, vice president of NAHA (see page 84), in December 1993 one could buy a pair of hedgehogs from a reputable source for $500. Now, depending on a number of variables (age, sex, size, and color), the typical price range is $1,500 to $3,000 a pair. A breeding pair brings a breathtaking $4,500. And, if they are pure white (in the trade these are dubbed snowflakes), add a thousand dollars!

You should beware, however, for as Mr. Frechette also states: "Some breeders have been inbreeding and using inferior stock. Unethical or unknowledgeable breeders are a problem and a big concern of ours."

How Many Hedgehogs Can You Keep?

Hedgehogs are solitary animals that actively hunt insects at dusk and after dark. Youngsters soon leave their mothers in order to find their own territory. One can therefore consider it not unnatural or cruel to keep a single pet hedgehog.

If you have had no previous experience with our prickly friends it is indeed best to start with a single specimen only! If you should see a nursing mother with her litter in a pet shop, they must not be separated. If the young are already scurrying about, you can safely take the whole family, provided the journey is short and unstressful.

The experienced fancier will have no problems in keeping several hedgehogs, but each animal must have its own separate cage. If you

have no breeding ambitions, however, make sure that animals of opposite gender don't come in contact during their exercise sessions!

Several hedgehogs in a large cage would be looking for trouble! Each hedgehog has a large territory and will attack any intruders. A cage, any cage, can never be sufficiently large to hold more than one hedgehog, although several females can often be kept together for short periods.

A Prickly Ball in the Hands

A hedgehog unaccustomed to your hand or, especially, your scent, will roll itself into a ball as soon as you approach it. This is a natural reaction to possible danger, or a "better safe than sorry" attitude from the hedgehog's point of view, even though you have the best intentions. A hedgehog is indeed an animal "not to be handled without gloves."

If you pick up such a spiny ball you are likely to get painful pricks that could result in your dropping the animal! If you have no gloves, then use a piece of sacking or other soft material and pick up the animal with one hand on either side of its body and under its belly. You may still feel the spines, but they will do you no harm. Once the animal is used to you and your scent (and that will happen sooner than you might think) it will run, unrolled, onto your hand. The African pygmy hedgehog fits nicely into the cupped hand of an adult human.

Important: Before acquiring a hedgehog, check that you will not be breaking any local laws or regulations. Your pet shop manager should be able to supply you with the necessary information.

I cannot overstate, and therefore will mention one more time the importance of the ongoing commitment you are undertaking to maintain the animal's well-being. Your hedgehog will need care for 3 to 10 years, sometimes longer! Do not consider this too lightly.

Hedgehogs That Need Help

A Mother with Offspring

It can happen occasionally that you acquire a pregnant female hedgehog, or a new mother with a litter.

For a start, you must not separate the mother from her young. You should also not disturb them in the nest box, as an agitated mother may dump the young, or even eat them!

Despite the fact that hedgehogs are known for their fondness for milk, you should not give any to the mother. Cow's milk may cause diarrhea, which can sometimes be fatal. Mothers with babies are best given pure water in a dish about 2 inches (5 cm) deep. Further feeding information is given on page 42.

First Aid and Medical Care for Ailing Arrivals

A healthy hedgehog reacts to sounds and scents in the "normal" hedgehog manner, erecting its head spines and attempting to ram your hand. Weak or sick animals are sluggish, and can often hardly roll into a ball. They sleep a lot, even at night, when they are supposed to be on the go.

A healthy wild hedgehog is very active and will eat at least one third of its own body weight each day, but because a fully grown African pygmy hedgehog weighs only about 1 pound (0.45 kg), this will not be too difficult to maintain. It is understandable, though, that an animal that is 5 ounces (142 g) underweight is not well. The hedgehog may have had bad food, or too little of it, or it may have an internal problem such as diarrhea, or be infested with external or internal parasites.

Sick animals are easily shocked by sharp noises, such as those made by cigarette lighters, light switches, and so on. The sudden chiming of a clock, an alarm going off, or unusual noises on the television can also be stressful to the sick animal. Try to keep such noisy objects out of earshot of the patient, so that it is not unnecessarily stressed.

A hedgehog that is accidentally subjected to low temperatures, due to sudden frost, electricity failure, and so on, must be placed in a warm spot, but not in a warm water bath. A bath usually gives negative results. Aspen or pine bedding, or a combination of both, should be placed in the sleeping chamber. Do not disturb; hedgehogs prefer being alone. Babies, of course, should be left with their mother, preferably in a nest box at least 12 x 12 inches (30 x 30 cm) and 14 inches (35 cm) high.

The Hospital Cage

The hospital cage (an old aquarium is ideal) should have a layer of newspaper on the floor. The shelter is placed at one end, and a shallow dish of mealworms and another of water at the other

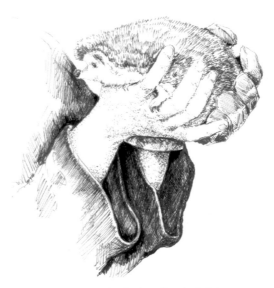

The African pygmy hedgehog fits nicely into the cupped hands of an adult human.

Although females can often be kept together for short periods, it is best to provide each hedgehog with its own cage. Remember that hedgehogs are solitary creatures in the wild.

end. Place the hospital cage in a quiet spot, at room temperature, that is at least 70.5°F (21.5°C). Do not place the cage next to a heater, or in a drafty or damp spot. In the case of hypothermia (especially in young animals), you can use a hot water bottle, securely packed in a cover, or bound with a towel, in the sleeping box. If you do not have a spare sleeping box, a shoe box will make a good substitute. Cut out an entrance hole 4 inches (10 cm) in diameter.

Emergency Feeding

Weak animals must be given food immediately. Cold youngsters that cannot help themselves should be wrapped in a soft cloth. Those that cannot feed themselves should be fed via a plastic pipette (or a bird feeder spout, available from pet shops). (For a good food recipe, see page 43.) At first you should feed the animal every hour. Do this calmly and systematically; it takes a long time, but do not try to hurry it or the animal might choke.

An amusing aspect of hand feeding juveniles is that the youngster will fall asleep in your hand as soon as it has had enough to eat. Once accustomed to it, the youngster will eagerly suck and lap at the tube. Then you can feed every two hours. At night, I give them a good feed once at 11 P.M., then again at 3 A.M. and 7 A.M. (See page 42 for further information.)

A Hedgehog Comes Home

Cleaning the New Arrival

The Bath

Because newly imported African pygmy hedgehogs were often dirty and untidy looking, an immediate bath and brush were essential. It is a well-known fact, however, that hedgehogs simply hate a bath, but there is sometimes no alternative. Fortunately this need not be done very often, but a bath twice a year (unless otherwise necessary) is highly recommended.

Start by running about 2 inches (5 cm) of lukewarm water, about 95.5°F (35.5°C), into a plastic bowl, and mix in a mild insecticidal dog or cat shampoo. Place the hedgehog in the bath and hold it with one hand (you will need a strong rubber glove). You must be firm, as the animal will undoubtedly begin to flounder and struggle. With your other hand, splash water all over its back. Do not forget its head, but try not to get water in its eyes, nose, or ears. Be absolutely certain to rinse it thoroughly. Then brush its spines from head to tail with a soft hairbrush.

After the bath, wrap the scared and somewhat bewildered animal in a dry towel so that most of the moisture is removed. Then place it in its cage on a layer of red cedar (this is because all parasites are rarely killed by a bath). If you use an insecticidal spray on the animal, cover its eyes, nose and ears with a cloth. Never use household sprays near the animals; as these can make them sick or even blind them if the spray gets into their eyes.

Eliminating External Parasites

In order to control external parasites, you must be able to examine the animal's belly (if it will allow you to). Wear rubber gloves (always disinfect after use). Do not turn the animal over, but hold it up above your head and examine it from below. If the animal is uncooperative, put it in a glass tank with a clean glass bottom so that you can then examine the underside. A flashlight will help you look for parasites, which will be easily seen if present.

In the "early days" a newly imported African pygmy hedgehog

Sturdy rubber gloves and a soft hairbrush are essential when you bathe a hedgehog. Fortunately, this need be done only a couple of times a year.

was, weather permitting, initially placed outdoors. This was done because the animal almost always had external parasites such as mites, ticks, and fleas. These must be immediately destroyed (see also page 46). In case you happen to come across recently imported or smuggled animals (they are no longer imported), I would recommend that they be regularly allowed to run outside. They should also be given red cedar bedding, the smell of which will drive away most of the parasites. You can also obtain a variety of insecticidal sprays of the type used for puppies and kittens. Ask for sprays that are safe for hedgehogs and for the environment.

Ticks: Ticks, which are extremely difficult to control with sprays, are best removed individually by hand. The following method is recommended: Place a drop of vegetable oil on each tick. After about five minutes you can remove the tick with a pair of tweezers. These parasites usually sit between the spines, and attach themselves to the hedgehog's skin with their piercing and gripping mouthparts. You must grip the tick as near to its head as possible, close to the hedgehog's skin, and remove it gently but firmly with a twisting motion. Make sure that the head of the tick is not left in the skin, as this can lead to secondary infections.

Unfortunately, ticks often are situated in very difficult spots among the spines, and to make things worse, the hedgehog may decide to roll up when you are working on it. But patience is usually rewarded, and if you try again a few days later you will eventually succeed. Small ticks that have burrowed right into the skin can often be overlooked, but after a few days of feeding they will become bloated with blood, dark in color and easier to find.

Important: Anyone unfamiliar with the hedgehog's anatomy can often

mistake its little, dark teats for ticks. If you are not completely sure what the tiny black spots are that you may have suddenly found on your hedgehog's underside, leave them for a few days. If they have increased in size, you can be sure they are ticks and can be removed as described above.

Maggots: Occasionally, newly imported hedgehogs develop small wounds or sores during their capture and transport. Close examination will often reveal an infestation of fly maggots in the wounds. Maggots are sometimes found in the ears, and youngsters may also be affected, especially those that have been abandoned by the mother. Sometimes such youngsters are badly weakened by large numbers of maggots. Fly eggs can be easily removed with the help of a clean paintbrush or toothbrush that is wiped between the spines. Maggots can also be removed in a similar manner.

Any open wounds must, of course, be handled with care. They should be washed with lukewarm water treated with a mild antiseptic. After treatment, dry the animal and place it in a warm spot or in its cage. Or, better still, take your pet to a veterinarian for treatment with potent new medications and advanced techniques.

Feeding Newly Acquired Hedgehogs

A newly acquired hedgehog, as I have just discussed, is first examined for parasites. If the animal is affected, then you must take immediate action. It is also important to provide the animal with drinking water and food. This should be done as soon as possible after you get the animal home. A dish of water (not milk!) and another dish of food should be placed in the cage. Make sure that the hedgehog finds the dishes. If you have acquired baby hedgehogs that are not yet on solid food, you must feed them as described

A slotted spoon or kitchen spatula makes a handy aid when you must lift a newly acquired hedgehog.

on page 44. You should, of course, study the whole feeding chapter of this book with care—including what is said about feeding adult hedgehogs.

Unfortunately, pet shops do not always provide their hedgehogs with an adequate diet, sometimes making do with canned cat food or similar products. You may also acquire a hedgehog from friends or acquaintances who, for some reason or other, do not want to care for their pets anymore. This often happens on the weekend when no pet shops are open.

What do you do then, when you acquire adult or juvenile hedgehogs and do not have adequate food for them? Or if you find an inadequately cared-for hedgehog in a pet shop where the manager is not yet fully aware of the hows and whys?

The first rule is: Never give frozen food, or food that comes directly from the refrigerator. Always give food at room temperature, or preferably a little warmer. Cold food can cause intestinal or stomach troubles, resulting in diarrhea.

Dog or cat food: The first emergency solution might well be dog or cat food. Most animal lovers have a dog or cat, and canned food is available in

most grocery stores. Dry dog or cat food can also be used, but should first be soaked in water until it is the consistency of thick soup. I have known some hedgehogs that would eat the dry food as is but, of course, fresh drinking water must always be available.

Meat: Frozen meat must always be thoroughly thawed before use. It can be thawed quickly by placing it in a plastic bag and suspending it in hot water. Only use lean meat and cut it into tiny pieces or, preferably, mince it. My hedgehogs get 1 ounce (28 g) of fresh lean meat daily, never more than this.

Because boned meat is low in calcium and magnesium, a mineral supplement is recommended to furnish the necessary requirements of these minerals. Red meat is also high in phosphorus, which makes the relative lack of calcium all the more troublesome.

Eggs: Eggs are a welcome addition to the diet, but give them sparingly. Do not give them raw. Only chopped, hard-boiled eggs should be used.

Fruit: A variety of fruit may also be given. Hedgehogs are especially fond of bananas. I give mine a piece of banana daily after their main meal (see page 42).

Mealworms: Mealworms are a very important part of the hedgehog's diet. They may be purchased from bait stores or some pet shops. However, do not think that mealworms are the staple diet of hedgehogs. I regard them as an important supplement; however, they, too, lack adequate calcium in relation to their phosphorus content.

Offering food: Every hedgehog will not immediately fall upon the food you offer it, especially if it is not yet accustomed to you and its new surroundings. Place the food and water in its cage and leave the animal in peace, so that it can decide what it wants to do. Its hunger will eventually overcome its shyness. If the animal has not eaten anything by the following day, it should be taken to a veterinarian. Refusal of food is a sign that the little animal is sick and requires treatment. Never wait too long before seeking professional help from your veterinarian.

The Day After Arrival

On pages 56–72 I discuss the adult weights of the various hedgehog species, together with some weights for growing juveniles. A newly arrived hedgehog should be weighed as soon as possible. An ordinary kitchen scale can be used for this purpose, and it will be quite easy to clean afterward. Weigh the animal weekly and keep a record of the weights. An increase in weight is good, but a loss is not desirable. It is sometimes necessary to know the exact weight to work out medicine dosages.

Stool samples: It is advisable to send a sample of the newly acquired hedgehog's feces to the veterinary laboratory for examination. Such an examination will reveal if internal parasites are present, and steps can then be taken to eradicate them. It is a simple matter to take a stool sample: take up a small amount of feces (about the size of a marble), place it on a piece of aluminum foil or in a plastic bag, and wrap it up neatly. Place in the refrigerator. Take a sample each day for three days and place a date label on each one. Then take them to your veterinarian. Never put feces samples from different animals together. If you have several hedgehogs, each will have a different name or number, which must be recorded along with the date on the label, to avoid possible confusion.

The Veterinarian

Most would agree that the hobby of keeping hedgehogs occasionally involves the treatment of sick animals, something that can cost a lot of

Use your bare hands only when you have been fully accepted by your pet; and then, scoop it up carefully from underneath.

money, because only the veterinarian can help you. A newly purchased hedgehog should be healthy and full of pep, and most of those seen in pet shops usually are. However, it is highly recommended that you consult a veterinarian if any of the following occur:

• Your hedgehog fasts for more than two nights.

• Your hedgehog suddenly loses its appetite, even though it previously ate the offered food with apparent relish.

• Your hedgehog has diarrhea for longer than one day (thin, greenish-colored, sometimes bloody feces).

• Your hedgehog coughs up blood.

• Your hedgehog frequently vomits, bringing up blood.

• Your hedgehog "sneezes" blood through its nostrils.

• Your hedgehog limps, wavers, or staggers, when fully awake on its normal rounds (for safety's sake, check that the temperature of the surroundings is at its minimum of 70.5°F [21.5°C].

• Your hedgehog is injured, or has an ulcer or abscess.

21

Care and Management

Accommodation for Hedgehogs

Wild hedgehogs, including the African pygmy hedgehog, are extremely active animals, and must never be kept in too small a cage. As far as I am aware, however, hedgehogs cannot be "potty trained," so you will most likely not want to give them the run of the house.

Hedgehogs generally sleep for most of the day and become active in the evening. In spite of this, I have known many hedgehogs that have been more or less active during the day, especially if food and water are available to them. I am sure that most hedgehogs can be "switched over" to daylight living once they get to know their owners and surroundings, and the necessary food is available.

Hedgehogs in Your Garden

On page 22 I discuss how you can allow several hedgehogs to run in the garden for a few hours a day under your supervision. One thing that you may be concerned about is the swimming pool, the fishpond, or the birdbath. You could, of course, completely cover your swimming pool in order to prevent your curious pets from falling in. Hedgehogs are adept swimmers, so if one should dive into the swimming pool, or somersault into the birdbath, there is no cause for immediate alarm as long as it has a way to climb out again. You can affix a number of small ladders around the edge of the swimming pool, and a few flat stones in the birdbath or pond will make it easy for a hedgehog to climb out.

Of course, you could fence off part of the garden for your hedgehog, especially if you have just one. You can keep the animal's box cage outside, but it must have a waterproof roof covered with asphalt roofing shingles or similar material. The exercise area can be as large as you like, but remember that hedgehogs can burrow well. You should therefore bury corrugated iron in the ground to a depth of about 24 inches (60 cm) around the perimeter of the run, to prevent escapes.

You can make the area attractive by planting shrubs or similar plants and the hedgehog will like to snuffle around them. To help keep the animal active, you can hide a few extra tidbits around the enclosure in addition to the usual food and drink dishes. This will encourage the hedgehog to "go hunting."

In warmer climates, such as parts of southern California or Florida, hedgehogs can stay outside all year, but in colder areas they must be brought indoors in the early fall. Animals kept outside will tend to hibernate in their sleeping box during colder spells. This is no cause for worry as long as you know the animal is healthy and well fed, and that food is available as soon as it awakes. You should regularly weigh your hedgehog with a kitchen scale throughout the year (see page 42), and if the animal should lose weight it will be best, perhaps, to take it to a warmer spot indoors and feed it. Outdoor hedgehogs must, of course, be checked frequently for external parasites and treated as necessary.

If you have a pool, it would be wise to improvise a few small ramps or ladders that will enable your pet to find its way back to dry land.

Temperature

If you intend to keep your hedgehog indoors then it is very important to realize that the box cage, whatever it is constructed from, must be neither too warm nor too drafty. You can easily detect the latter by lighting a candle or a stick of incense and holding it at various positions near the cage. Any drafts will be revealed by the direction of the flickering. Do not use this method inside the cage. Place the cage in a spot where there are no drafts.

Important: Be careful not to ignite the extremely flammable bedding with the open flame.

The cage should never be placed near a radiator or other heating apparatus, however good it may look! Remember that in the wild, the African pygmy hedgehog will sleep in its burrow to avoid the heat of the day, only emerging at night when the temperature is cooler. Overheating can result in a heart attack or other maladies.

The temperature should not be too low either. A constant temperature of 70.5°F (21.5°C) would be ideal, but as it is always colder close to the floor it is acceptable that a minimum of 66.5°F (19°C) will give the hedgehog no problems. You can read the correct temperature by placing the thermometer on the floor.

Sounds

Hedgehogs have an excellent sense of hearing (see page 78) and can perceive sounds that are too high for the human ear. High-frequency, whistling noises provoke a shock reaction, and should be avoided. The tinkling of glass, the flicking of a light switch, the sometimes unusual tones from the radio and television, even the clucking of a tongue—all are sounds that the hedgehog, even a tame one, cannot abide. Its reaction is to erect the forehead spines immediately.

Exercise

Exercise is important to hedgehogs. I have, unfortunately, seen many hedgehogs that have been kept for too long in cages that were much too small for them. Within a year, such hedgehogs will become crippled or have difficulty in walking—disabilities similar to those caused by bad diet! An adequate exercise area (see page 27 for minimum size) is thus essential.

Nails: If the hedgehog does not have the opportunity to run in the garden, its nails may grow too long and malformed. In such cases, a trip to the veterinarian is necessary. Plenty of exercise will prevent this.

Climbing: As hedgehogs are excellent climbers, and your pet will want to practice its talents, make sure you have adequate fencing around the exercise enclosure. You can give it extra climbing exercise by providing ladders leading to the top of its box cage, so that it can climb up one side and perhaps roll off the other!

Free play outdoors: When you let your pet run in the garden, you must keep a close eye on it and watch where it goes. Hedgehogs snuffle around all over the place, and will get under your feet before you know what's happening. So beware! Tame hedgehogs will follow you all over the house (and garden) like a dog. They will know you by your scent.

Indoors or out, heavy, shallow glass or ceramic dishes make excellent food and water dishes for your hedgehog.

A fenced yard is an ideal place for your hedgehog to exercise.

If your yard is not enclosed, careful supervision will be necessary.

Hidden tidbits will encourage your pet to go "hunting."

Chances are good that it will also find its own live insect prey.

HOW-TO:
The Hedgehog Cage

The best type of cage is a box, which is quite easy to make yourself. The height is 12¾ inches (32 cm), the length 24 inches (60 cm) and the width 13¾ inches (35 cm). You can use ½ inch (1.5 cm) plywood, chipboard, or pine planks, the latter being the most expensive. The floor and lower half of the walls of the cage should be given several coats of good quality epoxy resin or polyurethane paint to prevent the absorption of urine. Remember, of course, that this must be completely dry (give it at least a week, maybe more) before a hedge-hog is introduced. This coating will make cleaning much easier.

As you can see in the drawing, the roof of the cage is removable and has a number of ventilation holes. An entrance hole 4 × 5 inches (10 × 13 cm) is made in one of the walls. The sleeping box is placed in a corner opposite to the entrance. This enclosure is 8 inches (20.3 cm) high, 9.5 inches (24 cm) long, and 6 inches (15 cm) wide; also with an entrance hole 4 × 5 inches (10 × 13 cm). The sleeping box should either be hinged or open on the bottom so that it can be cleaned (frequently).

You can make a small door over the entrance hole, so that the hedgehog can be allowed out for a run in your living room or den. The water and food dishes are best placed outside the cage on the floor, but some fanciers like to place them in the cage. Newspapers and bedding should be changed at least every second day. A hedgehog will stay healthiest if, in addition to adequate food and drink, it has a clean home.

The actual sleeping box can be made of wood, but you could also improvise temporarily with a cardboard shoebox or similar item. This must, of course, be renewed at intervals as it gets soiled, and occasionally a hedgehog will gnaw at the edges of the box. The box is placed without its lid upside down on the floor of the cage. A shoe box is just about the right size for a hedgehog sleeping box, which should never be too large. Enough room for the animal to stretch out is all that is required. The hedgehog sleeps either stretched out or rolled up.

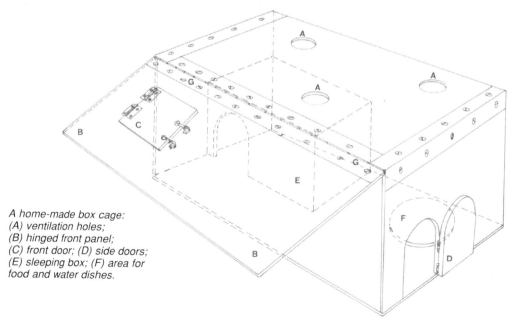

A home-made box cage:
(A) ventilation holes;
(B) hinged front panel;
(C) front door; (D) side doors;
(E) sleeping box; (F) area for food and water dishes.

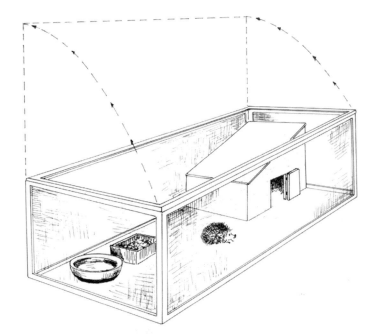

A satisfactory cage can also be made of wire mesh. The sleeping box should be wooden, however, as the hedgehog feels more secure with a "roof over its head."

Bedding should be provided so that the hedgehog is warm and cozy. Hay or dry leaves, which are used as bedding by many fanciers, are not ideal as they do not absorb enough moisture from the urine and droppings, leaving the sleeping box wet, messy, and smelly. The best bedding to use in the sleeping box is a layer of newspaper, with pine or cedar bedding on top; aspen, which has recently become popular as bedding for small animals, can also be used.

The Exercise Area
As has already been shown, hedgehogs are active animals and, in the wild, are really "on the go" for most of their waking hours. It is therefore obvious that a pet hedgehog's exercise area can never be too large. The more room it has to putter and snuffle around in, the happier and healthier it will be.

One way to provide a general exercise area is to make an enclosure about 6 × 9 feet (1.8 × 2.7 m) around the cage. The wall of the enclosure should be of plywood or some other smooth material, and not less than 15 inches (38 cm) high because hedgehogs can climb quite well. If you use wire mesh, you will have to turn in the top of the wire horizontally about 6 inches (15 cm) to keep the animal from climbing out. The exercise area should also be covered with a layer of newspaper and topped with a good quality bedding.

Old carpet or similar leftover material is unhygienic, but you can have a piece of linoleum under the newspaper and bedding to further protect the floor.

The Food and Water Dishes
The glass lids of preserving jars make excellent food and water containers. If you do not have these, then shallow earthenware, porcelain, or glass dishes should be used. These are heavy, and cannot be tipped over by the animals. Plastic dishes are generally not suitable because they are too light. Glass is the easiest to keep clean.

If you have several hedgehogs and each has its own cage and run, then it follows that each must have its own food and water dishes. If your hedgehogs have the run of the backyard, each must have its own food and water dishes in order to avoid quarrels.

An African pygmy hedgehog checking out a tall tuft of grass.

House Training

The question "Is it possible to housetrain a hedgehog?" must be answered with an emphatic "No." Healthy animals defecate two or three times per day. The droppings are firm in texture and can be picked up with toilet paper. Unfortunately, in my experience, it is impossible to know precisely where Prickles is going to deposit its droppings! If the animal has the run of the house, do not be surprised to find droppings under the radiator, under a cupboard, behind the desk, or even in an open vase!

The latter happened often at my home. One of my hedgehogs had the habit of climbing up a 1 foot (30.5 cm) high earthenware vase and there, like a sailor in the rigging, would observe what was going on in the room. After a few minutes he would get down and continue his explorations. A bit later

we could smell the "well-known scent," but did not know precisely where to look until our beagle stuck his nose in the vase and gave us a clue! The hedgehog used that vase many times thereafter.

Hedgehogs also urinate anywhere they happen to be. They set their legs apart so that the belly does not get wet. For safety's sake you must lay down newspapers when the hedgehog is loose in the house. It can also happen that a hedgehog will step in its own droppings and then scurry about with dirty feet, another reason for laying down newspapers! It is therefore clear that when the hedgehog is free in the house you must keep an eye on it, and clean up as necessary before there are any unpleasant accidents.

Hedgehogs can be trained to use a small litter pan in there own enclosure. Obtain a tray that is about one foot square, and fill it with litter to a depth of approximately two inches (5 cm). Clean the pan daily and change all of the litter a couple of times a week.

Breaking the Nocturnal Habit

Although hedgehogs are naturally nocturnal animals, it is possible to train them to be active during the day and to "go to bed with us" at night. You will not have much pleasure from an animal that is only active in the evenings and when you are asleep. As with hamsters, it is possible to break the nocturnal habit, but it must be done gradually. You must feed the animal at a later time each night over a period of several days. My hedgehogs are fed at 7 A.M., and again at midday. In the evening, they get fresh water and a few tidbits only. They stay awake many hours during the day and in the evening, and fall into a deep sleep at 11 P.M., exhausted from a day of pleasure.

Banishing Boredom

Being naturally energetic animals, hedgehogs must not have their activity suppressed. Only an active animal will stay healthy. One that gets just its food and drink will become lazy, fat, and eventually infirm. A hedgehog with nothing to do will become restless, feel sorry for itself, and eventually become indifferent.

As soon as something unusual happens in the room, a healthy hedgehog pricks up its ears and runs away. An active hedgehog hates boredom. Hedgehogs are markedly inquisitive and snuffle with their funny little

A few fresh sprigs scattered on your deck will give your pet something to investigate.

pointed snouts into every nook and cranny, under every cupboard and behind every magazine rack. They find leather objects especially attractive. Leather chairs are sniffed, licked and, if possible, gnawed. The hedgehog's sharp little teeth most often attack the spot where the leather is attached to the frame.

Toys: Leather or rawhide "chews" made for puppies are suitable for hedgehogs as well, and can be purchased in pet shops and supermarkets. Your hedgehog will find these a good substitute for the leather lounge, and the toys will help persuade it to behave itself.

Heavy paper: Large paper grocery bags (paper only, not plastic!), heavy wapping paper, and old clean rags will also make good play items. I don't need to tell you that the bottom shelf in my bookcase is protected with a sheet of plywood! A hedgehog once "disappeared" inside a magazine rack and, in no time at all, had rendered my newspapers and magazines unreadable! Hedgehogs like to make a play nest with the shreds. If a hedgehog were to go unnoticed into the encyclopedia set in your bookcase, it would be an expensive matter!

In the absence of anything better, newspapers can be given to help relieve boredom. These will be ripped to shreds and made into a pyramid-shaped play nest in some corner. If you clean up with a broom or vacuum when the hedgehog is in the area, do not be surprised if it attacks the appliance and bites it as if to "shake it to death," just like a hound shakes its prey. Only in this case there is no danger; all you see is an angry, trembling hedgehog—an exceedingly funny sight, believe me!

Biting

When alarmed, or if unaccustomed to you, a hedgehog can suddenly (and painfully) bite. And not only on your hand, but also on your foot or ankle. This biting can be a sign of fear, defense, or even hunger. A biting hedgehog does not let go too quickly either, a sign of the kind of animal it is. Hedgehogs are insectivorous and once an invertebrate victim is caught in the mouth it is held tightly until it is exhausted. If a hedgehog bites your finger or foot, you should therefore not try to shake it off because that will encourage the animal to hang on all the more! After a while it will let go itself. This does not sound very nice, but that is the way it is!

Important: If you are bitten, see your doctor immediately. (See page 85.)

New hedgehogs should be handled with care, preferably using protective gloves. Once accustomed to you and its new quarters, the hedgehog will no longer be aggressive.

Mother and Offspring

Hedgehog breeding is becoming popular in the United States, and you may have occasion to buy a gravid female. Sooner or later you will thus have a litter of youngsters to care for. If you notice that the female is pregnant, or if she has young, it is important to inspect her cage and run. Is it clean? Is there enough of the right food? (See page 42.) Is the temperature correct? (See page 23.) Does the whole family fit in the sleeping box? If not, you must quickly give them a larger one. The young creep close to the mother, but if there are a lot of them, there may not be enough room. Then there may be a possibility that one or more of the weaker young are not kept warm enough.

Hand Rearing

If, in spite of an adequate sleeping box, it seems that some youngsters are being inadequately reared, then it will be necessary for you to hand rear them. Don't be too eager to try this! It is not easy, and can take a lot of time. First, observe the whole family carefully, especially when they are all sleeping together. (The sleeping box should have a removable lid.) Do not pick up or touch the youngsters, or you will leave your scent on them, upsetting the mother who could bite the young or throw them out of the nest box.

Youngsters that are thrown out or neglected are usually suffering from hypothermia. Place each animal in a separate box or basket, on a layer of newspaper covered with bedding, on which has been placed a hot water bottle wrapped in a towel. The warmth must be comfortable—72° to 82°F (22°–28°C). The animal is loosely covered with a woolen blanket or another towel. Check the bottle regularly and refill it with warm water when necessary. Personally I refill the bottle every five hours, including nighttime. (For hand feeding instructions, see page 42.)

Note: At some point the mother will start puffing at the young. This is a sign that she wants nothing more to do with them. In other words, they are now independent and should be housed separately.

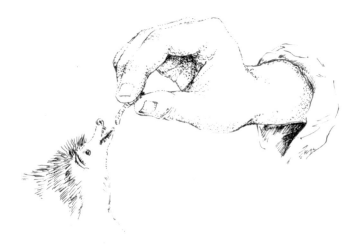

A tempting tidbit will help you win your new pet's trust.

Tame Hedgehogs

Hedgehogs have not really been with us long enough to say that they are domesticated in the same sense as cats, dogs, rabbits, and hamsters. At the present time newly acquired hedgehogs may be from a first or second generation captive breeding, but most are wild captured, imported animals.

Your first encounter with your pet, therefore, may well be a not particularly friendly one. The hedgehog will likely be distrustful and scared. It may roll itself up when you come close, may puff threateningly or attempt to butt you with the erected spines on its forehead,

or it may try to run away. Fortunately, this behavior does not usually last long and, in a few days, its behavior will change for the better. Hedgehogs already accustomed to humans will get to know you even faster.

My Tip: To break the ice between you and your new friend, hold a mealworm in front of its nose.

Hedgehogs and Other Pets

It has been shown that most household pets will quickly get used to the addition of a hedgehog to the family, and we have never had any difficulties with our animals. Once your dog is properly trained, it will leave the hedgehog alone, except perhaps giving it the occasional friendly sniff. Obviously, you must be present when the animals are first introduced and must be strict with the dog and remove it if the hedgehog begins to puff or vomit. Our beagle shares his food dish with one of the hedgehogs!

The first reaction of a cat, when confronted with a hedgehog for the

Once your cat feels the sharp spines of a hedgehog, it is not likely to repeat the experiment.

first time, is often to cautiously tap the newcomer with the paws. This is especially true with kittens. It is only a sportive gesture and need not worry you; when the cat comes in contact with the prickles it will think twice about repeating the action. Most hedgehogs roll themselves up quickly but can sometimes suddenly ram the unsuspecting cat with their spines! The cat will then soon seek out a "safe" place!

Today, rabbits are often kept as household pets. Hedgehog and rabbit usually get on very well together. They sniff each other and sometimes a hedgehog will bite at a passing rabbit, pulling out a bit of fur and triumphantly carrying it back to its nest.

Guinea pigs and hamsters are very nervous animals and are thus not recommended as companions for hedgehogs.

Vacations

Hedgehogs eat well and are active. If you have a large hedgehog pen, it is possible to stay away for as long as a day. Before you go, make sure that the run is clean, that fresh water is available, and that there is adequate food. Young hedgehogs that you are still rearing cannot be left alone, but if they are independent you can feed them before you go. When you return in the evening, you must again supply fresh water and food.

If you are going away for more than one day, you must get a reliable friend or acquaintance to look after your hedgehogs. He or she must be told precisely what has to be done: how often to clean out the cage and run, how much and when to give food and water, when and for how long to give it exercise, and so on. Give that person the name, telephone number, and address of your veterinarian in case of emergency. Ideally, your helper should come a few days before you go away to learn the routines of care and so that sitter and pet can get to know each other. Do not forget to leave your vacation address and phone number.

If it is impossible to arrange for a friend to stop by regularly to care for your pet, you might have to consider moving your hedgehog—cage and all—to the house or apartment of a potential caretaker. Naturally, this is not recommended. Whenever possible it is best to leave your pet in its familiar surroundings. Should this not be a viable option, spend at least an hour with your pet in its temporary home.

Vacation Checklist

When you are going to be away for any length of time, be sure to provide all of the following items:
- The hedgehog's own cage or tank, and nest box—all carefully cleaned.
- The familiar brand of bedding.
- The animals own food and water dishes.
- Sufficient food (and don't forget the feeding schedule!).
- The veterinarian's name, address, and telephone number.
- Finally, remember to call in regularly.

This puppy and hedgehog appear to have decided that toleration and respect is the best policy.

Raising Your Own Hedgehogs

By Pat Storer

Hedgehogs will not breed and have babies unless you respect them, simulate their natural environment, keep them parasite free and give them food that they like and can thrive on.

If you do all the above, you may become a successful hedgehog breeder. You will be able to follow the complete life cycle of an evolutionarily successful little creature that has survived thousands and thousands of years with little change—ones that were around during the days of T-Rex and beat the system and survived! You will be able to observe firsthand the primitive courtship of the insatiable, persistent little males. You will see the female swell and become chubby with babies during her short pregnancy. You will hear the first barely audible, yet unmistakable squeaks of life as the 1 inch (2.5 cm) long, naked babies are born and search for their mother's nipple. You will be able to handle and marvel at these same babies a few days afterward while their spiny coats are still soft. You will be able to inspect their naked pink faces and feet when they resemble a strange, yet adorable little alien creature. In all, you will be able to take an undeniably intimate peek into the life cycle of this wonderful little animal, another of nature's marvels. And you can do all of the above in less time than you can imagine.

Living Quarters

Breeding hedgehogs must be housed separately, except during the actual breeding. Giving each one its own home after it is an adult works the best. For adult breeders, which should be kept separately, small airline-type animal crates about 16 inches high × 13 inches wide, × 23 inches long (41 × 33 × 58.5 cm) work best. This size is perfect for the small varieties of hedgehogs. The nice thing about plastic/fiberglass crates is that they are easily washed and disinfected. Some brands even come in decorator colors.

I use clean wood shavings from pine or aspen about 1 inch (2.5 cm) deep for bedding in all containers. Be sure they are from untreated wood— no penta-cote or creosote. Do not use cedar bedding in these types of containers as the vapors could be harmful to your animals.

Be sure the room the hedgehogs are in is well ventilated and protected from direct sun and air conditioner drafts.

For breeding hedgehogs, I recommend that you do not use a litter pan. Pine or aspen bedding is absorbent and the feces and moist material can be removed daily. The container can be completely changed and disinfected as necessary. The litter pan usually gets in the way of breeding animals and reduces the room especially for females with babies.

The Sleeping Chamber

To give it the feeling of security it craves, the mother will need a nesting chamber, although some females will prefer to have their babies outside of the chamber. You may cut a 10 × 12 inch (25.4 × 30.5 cm) length of thin-walled PVC sewer pipe (nonperforated because babies can get stuck in the holes). Push a PVC cap on one end so they can feel they are at the end of their own little tunnel. I do not glue the cap on. Place the open end into the crate first. The animals will feel more secure if the capped end is the one that points to the door of the crate, shielding them from visual distractions, drafts, light, and traffic. If you have to inspect the animal(s) you can gently remove the tube, look inside, and if necessary tip it until the animal(s) slides out.

Some females will drag or carry sawdust in the tube when they are about to deliver and others will take every piece of shaving out of the tube. Most of the time hedgehogs will sleep curled up in the tube head first. But almost always, when they have new babies, they will keep their head pointed to the open end of the tube for a short time. Always be sure the open end is toward the back of the crate when they are due to have babies so they have privacy and seclusion.

Planning the Breeding

Several factors should be considered when picking animals to mate. The number of babies in the litter is determined by the dam, and the sex of the offspring is determined by the sire of the litter. Therefore, offspring (both males and females) should be kept from females that produce large litters and bring them to weaning age. Other factors are to be considered when picking potential breeding stock. Just buying hedgehogs does not ensure you of the most for your money. Because both males and females carry genes for all inherited traits, keep records to ensure you of the best potential parents of future litters. Pick offspring from the following:

- Dams that produce large, healthy litters.
- Sires that have consistent, reliable libido.
- Parents that have strong immune systems (high resistance to skin and other diseases).
- Parents that have gentle temperaments.
- Parents with good conformation.
- Mothers with good nurturing instincts.

A non-pregnant female has a flat belly. The vaginal orifice is very close to the anus (right). The male's penis is the swelling where you would expect the navel to be (left).

When to Breed

I begin all breeding at feeding time. When I plan to breed a female, I remove the pipe and litter pan from the female's crate. Leaving them in will give a very shy female a place to retreat. I then gently slide the male into the female's crate.

The Courtship

Normally, courtship, at least on the male's part, begins immediately. If you want to observe, get yourself a chair, relax, and you will observe an interesting and entertaining courtship ritual.

Few females are receptive immediately, and play more than hard-to-get. The male cautiously approaches the now-vibrating, hissing, and puffing living pin cushion. His plaintive squeaks are unmistakably intended to please and entice her as the persistent little male nudges and pushes against her, trying to caress her. The more she resists, the harder he tries to win her over.

A young male hedgehog.

An old European riddle goes something like this: Question: How do hedgehogs make love? Answer: Very carefully!

If the female is not receptive, she eventually tires of the male's endless advances. At this point, she will stick her head out and either scurry off, or

A mature male hedgehog.

A young female hedgehog.

turn and face him, forehead quills projecting forward like some ancient triceratops. In this latter case, she will butt him with great force in the side. He is shielded by his own cover of impenetrable quills, now crisscrossed in a multitude of directions to protect his skin and feelings. Some males will still persist in their advances, now that the female's underside is not tightly curled. Most males, especially experienced ones, eventually will win the female over.

Length and Frequency of Breeding

I normally leave the males and females together for two nights so they can have ample time to get to know each other. Even the most resistant female will drop her guard eventually. After 48 hours, I return the male to the crate, after monitoring both of them throughout the breeding for any possible injuries. I post on each of their crates the dates bred and to whom, as well as a projected birth date.

I wait two days.

I repeat the breeding process with each female again after the two-day wait and repeat both sessions for a total of four breedings. Gestation is 35 days. Never put a male in with a female that could be about to give birth. This would be a disaster, because they would both enjoy a twilight meal together—her babies!

This male and female have begun courting.

Checking for Pregnancy

By now, your females should be very gentle and you are used to them opening up on your hands. Gently palpate the tummy area with your fingertips. You can feel the more convex shape of the stomach area around the last week, and her nipples will be two distinct rows of pink buds, ready for the babies. This is why it is helpful to check your females often, so you get to know the normal nonpregnant feel of their abdomen, and can feel the difference. Tame females seem to enjoy this gentle probing of their body.

Birth and Care of the Family

I do not disturb a potential mother for at least five days prior and three days after the projected birth date. During those periods, quietly remove and replace food and litter pans. Listen carefully, with your ear next to the crate, and if there are babies, you will hear the unmistakable first squeaks of life. If you need to inspect the female during this period, gently remove the tube, being extra careful not to bump it. But even doing so with care may cause the mother to reject or eat her babies. *Do this only with that in mind.* Do not slide the female

During mating, the male cautiously mounts the female from behind.

out unless it is an emergency. When you hear the squeaks, or if she is remaining in her tube, and not eating, place the food dish in the back of the crate near the opening of her tube. Once you are sure there are babies, jot down the date of birth.

When you are sure you have babies born, you can pile up the shavings a bit so you can elevate the open end of the tube to keep the babies from rolling out and getting "lost." Check daily for a couple of days to see if babies are lost in the shavings. With the elevated open end method, I rarely have babies lost.

If you see a baby out of the tube (or in the case of a female that has her babies out of the tube you see a baby a distance away from the mom) gently lift the baby with a small spoon and place it in the tube or near the mother. This may have to be repeated a few times. If you decide to chance it, gently slide the mother out of the tube, place the baby and any others back in the tube, and gently mix them. Elevate the open end of the tube, and let the mother crawl back in on her own. In the event that a baby is "rejected" several times, mark it with a tiny dot with a permanent marker so you will know if it is the same baby or not. If it is the same baby, you may have to hand raise it.

If you could see a baby within a few hours of birth, you would find that they have no visible spines. The spines are under the top layer of succulent skin that quickly dehydrates the first day as the spines rapidly grow. Within five to twelve hours, the spines protrude through the skin. At this time they are white and pliable. The baby hedgehogs look like little cockleburs and are absolutely adorable.

Weaning Babies

Babies are weaned at four to six weeks depending upon the size of the youngsters. Large litters will tend to have babies that are smaller at weaning. Remember to increase the food ration in the crates that have litters, and watch to see if it is all consumed. When the babies are two to three weeks old they will venture from the nest and begin to sample mom's ration. Keep adequate food to ensure normal growth of the litter. When babies are about halfway between the size of a golf ball and a tennis ball, they are ready to wean if they are eating food well.

Babies raised in a crate with a litter pan will still use the litter pan when you move them to another container or sell them.

Records

Keep good records for animal size, fertility, libido, temperament, litter size, mothering instincts, and so on. Keep only females that produce the traits you want to continue producing. Keep males from parents of the same traits and also from males that settle females. If you want to build a nice productive herd, records are a must.

A young, healthy African pygmy hedgehog should put on almost 1¼ ounces (35 g) per week.

This female is being gently palpated to determine whether or not she is pregnant.

A few days after birth the babies are still blind and helpless.

Do not touch the babies unless they are orphaned or rejected by the mother.

Nursing babies will gain weight rapidly. At two to three weeks of age they will start sampling food from their mother's bowl.

Feeding Your Hedgehog

Do not place food and drink dishes in the sleeping box, nor in the box cage. Instead, place them outside the box cage. This encourages the hedgehog to go out "foraging." Good exercise after a night's sleep is important. Personally, I give my hedgehogs their food about an hour after they awaken and have sniffed and wandered for a while. Animals that have their food right in front of them when they awaken will start feeding immediately, and will soon become lazy and fat. A hedgehog must stay alert and active, otherwise it will become overweight.

A good menu will contain certain amounts of proteins, fats, minerals, and roughage. This last is necessary to maintain the function of the intestines, but it will have little or no nutritional value. Research has shown what ingredients are essential for hedgehogs, and these are listed on page 43.

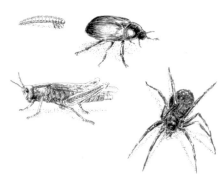

Although hedgehogs love mealworms (top left), their teeth are designed to crack insects: (clockwise) beetle, spider, grasshopper.

Feeding Juveniles

A healthy juvenile African pygmy hedgehog should put on about 1.25 ounces (35 g) per week. Avoid overfeeding, and monitor growth by weekly weighing. Full grown African pygmy hedgehogs weigh about 1 pound (0.45 kg).

My tip: Do not give moist food only. Hedgehogs' teeth are designed to "crack" insects, worms, and even young mice. Soft food on a daily basis will cause tooth scaling and gum infections.

Food must never be too cold (preferably room temperature), nor salted, smoked, or herbed. Hand fed juveniles should be given food with a temperature of about 95.5° F (35.5° C), which is the same as the body temperature.

Never give leftovers. Everything must be fresh and should not smell "off." Food (and water) dishes should also be washed and disinfected daily before being filled with fresh food. Finally, never give the following items, which are really taboo: candy, chocolate, cake, and milk and other dairy products. They will cause diarrhea. A little fruit may be given daily (apples, bananas, raisins), but give these only sparingly.

Feeding Independent Young and Adult Hedgehogs

Most fanciers feed their hedgehogs twice a day; one meal after they awake and another (somewhat larger) meal after the evening run, say an hour before bedtime.

I like to make up little balls of food for my hedgehogs and give them these in addition to a little dog or cat food, and about five mealworms per

Hedgehogs need protein, carbohydrates, fats, minerals, vitamins, and fiber. The more variety the better.

animal. I kill the mealworms by putting them in boiling water for a minute before giving them to the hedgehogs. You can give the mealworms live if you wish but you must use smooth glass bowls, otherwise the worms may get away. Weak hedgehogs requiring a boost can be fed single mealworms directly from your fingers. Just hold the mealworm in front of the animal's mouth, but be sure to wear gloves if you are dealing with adult hedgehogs!

Many hobbyists think that mealworms alone are an adequate diet for their hedgehogs, but that is far from the truth! Too many mealworms will make the hedgehog fat, lazy, and even sick. A diet consisting solely of mealworms will be deficient in calcium and too high in fat.

Moreover, there is the necessity of giving your animals something substantial to chew in order to properly maintain their teeth. Apart from what has already been recommended, you can offer chicken necks and hearts, and shrimp.

Water: Food provides the essential ingredients for growth and energy, but water is essential as well. Like all animals, hedgehogs must never be left

My recipe, which I have adapted from that of hedgehog expert Dr. W. Poduschka, is as follows:

- 14.25 ounces (400 g) of lean, finely minced meat (lean hamburger meat is fine)
- 1 teaspoon of vitamin-calcium supplement
- 1 teaspoon safflower or canola oil
- 4 teaspoons moist or dry cat or dog food (you can use each type alternately)
- ½ teaspoon boiled whole oats, rolled wheat, boiled brown rice, or triticale flakes

Mash the ingredients together with a fork, and roll the mixture into little balls of about 1 ounce (28 g). Place them on foil and freeze them. Once frozen, they can be stored in a plastic bag in the deep freeze.

Enough frozen balls for the following day's rations are placed in the refrigerator the evening before so that they will be thawed. When you take them out they will still be too cold to give directly to the animals. But, as I have already noted, I give my hedgehogs an hour in their run in the morning before they are fed, and this gives the food time to warm up to room temperature before they eat it. The same goes for afternoon or evening meals, but be sure to place the food in a safe place while it is warming up, especially if you have a dog or a cat!

Mealworms are best killed (by putting them in boiling water) before they are presented to the hedgehog.

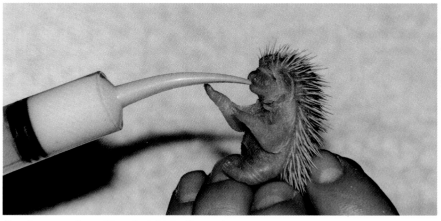

Feeding an orphan with a dental irrigation syringe.

without water. Vertebrate animals lose body water via the feces and urine, and by evaporation from the skin, lungs, and mucous membranes. More water is used inside the body for various metabolic processes. Plenty of good, clean water is important to keep the tissues in good order. Do not forget fresh water.

Nursing Babies

We all know that the birth of several young hedgehogs is a very exciting event; but please try to control your curiosity (and that of your friends and neighbors who suddenly discover a use for their video camera!) Mother hedgehog is very sensitive to disturbances at this time, especially from strangers. She and her babies should not be bothered!

It is absolutely taboo to pick up newborn or nursing youngsters in your hand! Your scent may cause the mother hedgehog to bite the disturbed youngsters or even throw them out of the nest! This does happen, so beware.

Place water and, twice a day, food dishes near the sleeping box (or should I say nursery?). Do this quickly and quietly. Give the mother the normal food described previously. Sometimes a weaker youngster may be forced out by its stronger siblings; it is best to hand rear such an animal (see below). After ten days, you can collect fecal samples from mother and babies to send to the veterinarian for parasitic examination.

Hand Feeding

Youngsters that have to be hand reared can still grow into normal adults. All you require is enthusiasm, patience, and time!

To feed the youngster you will require a good brand of infant formula, or one prepared for puppies or kittens. There are several commercial products readily available from veterinarians and pet stores.

The liquid food is best administered via an unbreakable plastic dropper or a kitten/puppy nursing bottle. After feeding, the utensils should be washed and sterilized.

The young animal is best taken in the hand and held belly upward for the feeding session. The open end of the dropper, or the bottle nipple is gently

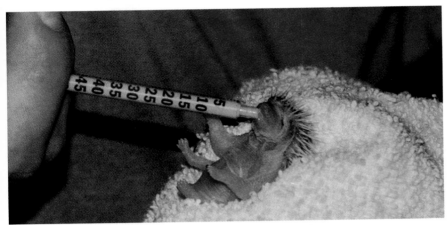

An unbreakable plastic eyedropper or pipette can also be used.

placed in the animal's mouth. At first you may find a few difficulties, but in most cases the baby will soon learn what is going on and will greedily suck up the mixture. Make sure that the opening in the pipette or nipple is not too large, or there may be a chance of the baby choking.

When the youngster has had enough, it falls asleep. Then, using a soft brush or a washcloth moistened with warm water, massage the belly and underside to help get digestion working well and to stimulate elimination. This action corresponds to the licking that the hedgehog mother typically does after nursing her young.

Young hedgehogs must be fed every other hour during the day, and every four hours at night. When they weigh about 2 ounces (58 g) you can introduce diluted baby food into the diet.

Important: Do not neglect to stimulate elimination. If you fail to do so regularly, a baby hedgehog's bladder can overfill and rupture.

My tip: I have had good results using semolina cereal thinned with water (not milk) and with honey and vitamins added. This is a second food for youngsters that are half grown. I also place a few snippets of lean red meat in the food so that the youngsters can practice chewing. Feces and urine can be cleaned off the body using a washcloth soaked in lukewarm water.

Young hedgehogs start to feed independently when their first milk teeth appear, though sometimes they may begin a few days earlier. In general, it can be stated that a young hedgehog weighing 2.75 to 3 ounces (78–85 g) should be eating solid food independently. For animals at this stage of development, I use dog biscuits, minced beef, and newly molted mealworms (thus still soft). Good quality, moist cat or dog food can be offered in a second dish.

Medical Care for Your Hedgehog

Sick Hedgehogs

Sick hedgehogs must be immediately transported to a veterinarian who is familiar with these animals. Do not attempt to treat the animal yourself. It should be placed in a warm spot in a sleeping box with a removable lid. If possible, have a friend accompany you to the veterinarian to carry the box, so that bumps and vibrations are kept to a minimum. The veterinarian won't be able to do much with an animal that is carsick on top of everything else.

Parasites

Newly imported hedgehogs are sometimes infested with parasites. However, you can rest assured that hedgehog parasites are not dangerous to people or other household pets, and will give you no problems provided your personal hygiene and care of other pets are adequate. Nevertheless, an infested hedgehog must be treated immediately (see page 19).

Your pet may be parasitized externally, internally, or both. External parasites can usually be discovered by simple visual inspection, but internal parasites are more difficult to detect. For the latter, you must collect a stool sample for microscopic examination by a veterinarian (see page 21). Only when the doctor has identified the problem, can a suitable recommendation for treatment be made. A hedgehog should have an annual checkup, and if the animal spends any time out of doors this should include a stool sample.

External Parasites

Weakened animals are subject to the worst infestations of external parasites, but healthy animals are not necessarily immune from attack. Several kinds of pests can infest hedgehogs.

Fleas: Normally only specialized flea species live on hedgehogs, but if you have other pets, such as cats or dogs, it can happen that their fleas will get on your hedgehog too. But they will only stay for a short time until they realize their mistake, then they will search for their home animal! To get rid of fleas, you can use a flea powder or an aerosol spray intended for puppies and kittens. Be very careful when applying these potentially toxic preparations. Follow the instructions for use exactly.

The nest and surroundings must be treated at the same time as the animal. Take out the bedding material and destroy it (preferably by burning). Then powder or spray the cage and sleeping box, being sure not to miss any nook or cranny where fleas, larvae, or eggs may be hiding.

A flea's life cycle is complete in about five weeks, and its eggs are not necessarily laid on the hedgehog. Untreated flea eggs, on the floor of the cage for example, will hatch into larvae that will develop into adult fleas ready to reinfest the animals.

Flea infestations are at their worst in the warmer summer

months. Bad infestations, with thousands of fleas, cause a hedgehog great distress, and can produce possible anemia through blood loss. Serious infestations are best treated by a veterinarian.

Mites: Mites are less likely than fleas to infest hedgehogs. It is easy to distinguish mites from fleas, as they do not jump but crawl about and are relatively larger. The whole life cycle of the mite takes place on the hedgehog, causing it considerable irritation. Mites also suck blood and, in severe infestations, it is possible for the hedgehog to lose some of its spines. Treatment is with flea preparations.

Ticks: Ticks are sometimes found on hedgehogs, especially newly imported ones. In tropical areas, ticks can transmit serious blood-borne protozoan infections. If you are not confident of your ability to remove ticks, get your veterinarian to do it. Don't necessarily trust other hobbyists with their "I-know-how-to-do-it" attitudes. If ticks are not removed properly, nasty secondary infections can develop. (Tick treatment is discussed in more detail on page 10.)

Fly larvae: Commonly known as maggots, these pests can occur in hedgehogs that have open wounds, sores, or ulcers. An infestation of maggots is known as *myiasis*. Some maggots produce a toxin that enters the bloodstream and can prove fatal.

Maggots are often found in or around the ear. They can be removed using a cloth or a cotton swab dipped in 30 percent alcohol or 3 percent hydrogen peroxide solution. The maggots will come quickly to the surface and can be picked out with sterilized forceps. If the maggots are in open wounds, then you cannot use alcohol or hydrogen peroxide. You must remove them with sterilized forceps, then treat the wound with an antiseptic salve. Large wounds or serious infestations of maggots must be treated immediately by a veterinarian.

Internal Parasites

Lungworms: Research, especially that carried out by E. Saupe, D.V.M., has shown that hedgehogs can have great problems with lungworms. For example, the worm *Crenosoma striatum* is widely found in European hedgehogs. Examinations of the feces of wild European hedgehogs found few animals that were not infected.

Lungworms can only complete their life cycle with the help of an intermediate host, in this case, one of various snail and slug species. My own examinations have convinced me that African pygmy hedgehogs are infected with a closely related lungworm. If you have hedgehogs in the garden, you should take regular stool samples to the veterinarian for examination, as there will probably be species of slugs or snails that can be intermediary hosts for lungworms.

I have been able to ascertain that these worms can encapsulate themselves in the lungs. Only really healthy hedgehogs are able to combat infestations of these parasites.

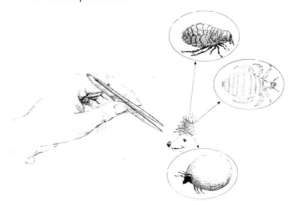

Various external parasites may attack your hedgehog: (clockwise from the top) flea, louse, tick (after a "full meal").

Observe your hedgehog carefully. A healthy animal is alert and curious. If your pet seems listless and lethargic, something may be wrong.

The life cycle of a lungworm is as follows: lungworm larvae contained in the feces of an infected host come free on the ground, attach and bore through the foot of a passing slug or snail, and go through two stages of development in the mollusk's body. Should a hedgehog eat an infested slug, the parasite stays in the new host's body and, after two more stages of development, becomes sexually mature and will multiply in the animal's lungs. The parasites then migrate out of the lungs into the intestines, where they are excreted with the stool.

Lungworm infestation is a severe condition, and, in spite of blameless husbandry, I have seen several hedgehogs die from them. Especially susceptible are weak, underfed, or late-born young. Mothers with late litters are also at risk. Fortunately, most captive pet hedgehogs are never fed with snails or slugs.

Unfortunately, there are no definite symptoms to suggest that an animal is infected with lungworms. But in the early stage of the infection, the hedgehog will begin to cough and wheeze. Later it will lose all of its appetite and quickly lose weight. Less commonly, it may continue to eat for a time, but will still lose weight. In general, the animal will appear to be short of breath and tired all the time.

An effective treatment is a double injection of 1 percent Citarin-L solution (Bayer) or equivalent, with an interval of two days between injections. Another remedy is Telmin-KH (Jansen), which comes in tablet form and can be administered by mixing it with food for five days. Fecal samples of the treated animals should be examined two weeks later to see if a second treatment will be necessary. The German biologist H. Fritzsche recommends a second treatment after two weeks for any hedgehogs that were badly infected; send fecal samples for examination two weeks after the second treatment. (Note: These treatments should be administered by, or under the direction of, a qualified veterinarian.)

Lung threadworms: These parasites are often found in hedgehogs that are already suffering from lungworms. Threadworms (*Capillaria* species) require no intermediate host, but research has shown that earthworms are capable of transporting the eggs. An infestation of these parasites must also be treated by a veterinarian. As a precaution, indoor hedgehogs should not be fed earthworms fresh from the garden.

Symptoms of lung threadworm infestation include coughing and wheezing. Lung threadworms can also be treated with Telmin-KH. Follow the instructions of your veterinarian implicitly. Don't think that by increasing the dosage the problem will be solved any faster! Three weeks after treatment, obtain a fecal sample for examination to determine if further treatment is necessary.

Intestinal threadworms (*Capillaria* species) are close relatives of lung threadworms. There are various species, none of which requires an intermediate host, though again the eggs may be transported by earthworms. Hedgehogs can continually reinfect themselves with these threadworms via their own droppings! The most effective preventive measure against infestation is to keep the hedgehog's area as clean as possible. Threadworms and their eggs are extremely tough, making an infestation hard to eradicate.

Infected animals will usually experience diarrhea, weight loss, and general debility. Treatment under the supervision of a veterinarian is necessary. Telmin-KH, finely crushed and mixed well with food, or 1 percent Citarin-L solution has been found effective. A second treatment is often necessary after two or three weeks. In any case, follow directions implicitly and submit a fecal sample for examination three weeks after the treatment.

Intestinal worms: *Brachylaemus* species of worms are often present in the intestines of newly captured wild hedgehogs. Seriously infested animals will be restless, will refuse to feed, and will quickly lose weight and become anemic. The animal should be treated immediately by a veterinarian. Telmin-KH, in the same manner as for intestinal threadworms, appears to be effective.

Coccidia (*Isospora* species) are small, round, parasitic protozoa that are highly resistant to cold, dampness, and even frost. In the native habitat of the African pygmy hedgehog they are not common, but in cooler areas hedgehogs are regularly infested. High temperatures and dry air will destroy the protozoa. Self-infection is possible. Serious infections result in bloody diarrhea. Veterinary treatment is required, and the cage must be cleaned out twice daily and the soiled bedding burnt. Entero-Sediv, in pellet form, and Paraxin powder (Boehringer) have been used with good results.

Other Conditions

Pneumonia: It is not surprising that an animal suffering from infestations of the two above mentioned parasites could quickly succumb to pneumonia, as the damaged lungs would soon allow a bacterial infection to take over. It is essential to consult your veterinarian for all medical problems.

Should a hedgehog suddenly develop runny eyes without other obvious symptoms, you should immediately take its temperature. (Special thermometers are available for small animals. Ask your veterinarian for advice.) If you find the animal is running a fever (see page 9), you will probably notice that the ears are not only warm to the touch but will be pink or red in color. If the animal develops weakness with labored, wheezing breathing or with a nasal discharge, there is a chance that it is suffering from pneumonia or some other respiratory infection.

With pneumonia the hedgehog's circulatory system is severely strained, and it is likely to die unless treated. You should consult your veterinarian immediately.

Eye infections: It is possible, given the hedgehog's active lifestyle, for particles of sand, dirt, and other foreign matter to get caught in its eyes. The African pygmy hedgehog can suffer especially when dirt gets trapped behind the *nictitating membrane*, a transparent third eyelid located beneath the outer lids at the outer corner of the eye. If the dirt is not removed an infection may develop, which if left untreated can lead to serious consequences. Also, an animal with foreign matter lodged in its eye will scratch constantly, with a high likelihood of further damage.

Continual scratching in the eye region will be a good indication that something is wrong. If you don't take heed, you may eventually notice that the animal has worn away some of the fur around the affected eye. Immediate attention is called for.

You can treat your pet by first rinsing the eye in warm water (an eyedropper works best, but you can improvise if you don't have one handy). After the rinse, you can apply an antibiotic eye lotion to help soothe the discomfort. Seek professional help without delay.

Eye infections can arise from causes other than mechanical irritation. A bacterial infection can develop, for example, if the hedgehog's resistance has been lowered by another disease, or by inadequate food, inferior housing and so on. Treatment often consists of the application of an aqueous ophthalmic solution or a petroleum based ointment as prescribed by your veterinarian.

It is usually necessary to apply the medicine for several days before the infection is cleared up. It cannot be stressed too strongly that the cage, sleeping box, bowls, and anything else used by the animal should be kept scrupulously clean when dealing with infectious diseases. And, as the ointment is quite sticky, and will pick up particles, it is best to forgo the normal bedding during the course of treatment. An old towel or similar item will make a good temporary substitute. The floor of the run must be cleaned as often as necessary.

Ailments of the ears: Fortunately, ear ailments are not very common. Should you notice a discharge from an ear, you should take the animal to a veterinarian. In a more serious stage of infection, the animal will paw at its ear. It may constantly tip its head to one side, and eventually may start running in circles. The veterinarian will probably prescribe antibiotics. At home, the most important thing will be to keep the animal's area clean, and, again, the normal bedding should be replaced by a towel until the crisis has passed.

Constipation: Many young hedgehogs die from constipation between the ages of eight and sixteen days. This often happens when commercial dry pellet foods are given to the mother. Should the youngsters also start to eat them, and if they don't get enough fluid from their mother, there is a danger of the pellets compacting in the intestines. Constipation will result. If you hold a sick youngster on its back, you will be able to see the discolored stomach through the skin and the anus may be enlarged to three or four times its normal size. If the stomach is not yet too discolored, there is still a good chance that the animal can be

saved. Offer it some fresh, juicy greens, pieces of apple, mealworms, raw meat, berries, milk of magnesia, and plenty of clean water. Do not neglect to consult your veterinarian!

It is not always food that causes constipation. Especially in adult animals, constipation can be caused by stressful circumstances. Prolonged transportation in a badly ventilated cage, or simply a change of location, are the two most common circumstances that might lead to stress-induced constipation. I have inspected shipments of African pygmy hedgehogs, directly arrived from Africa, in which 65 percent of the animals suffered from constipation due to dehydration from water deprivation during shipment.

Even the short journey from pet shop to home can stress the animal to the extent that it becomes constipated. It is, therefore, important that you inspect each newly acquired hedgehog for this problem.

If your hedgehog is indeed constipated, you will be able to tell quite easily by feeling its abdomen with your fingers. If the belly is hard and distended, and if the animal has not defecated within 30 minutes of its arrival in your home, then it is constipated. You can treat the condition immediately by giving eight to ten drops of milk of magnesia (depending on the size of the hedgehog) mixed with drinking water, using an ordinary medicine dropper. Check for droppings, and if none have been produced by the following day, call your veterinarian.

Pregnant females that are constipated can also be treated with milk of magnesia. Never, under any circumstances, use heavy oils such as castor oil. Experience has shown that with an adequate diet (such as that described on page 42) pregnant females and youngsters are not likely to become constipated. Hedgehogs that have plenty of room for exercise and an adequate diet will seldom, if ever, suffer from constipation. You must remain vigilant, however, and never ignore constipation, thinking that it will just go away. You must be prepared to treat the animal immediately. Constipation, and many other ailments, can kill small animals like hedgehogs quickly.

Diarrhea: Young hedgehogs, especially newly independent ones, often have the bad habit of eating more than is good for them. This results not in constipation, but rather in diarrhea. Animals with diarrhea that has no apparent cause can be given charcoal mixed in with their food. As diarrhea is often a symptom of one disease or another, it is advisable to consult a veterinarian, who will diagnose the problem and prescribe a treatment to combat the intestinal infection.

Tooth deposits and gum infections: The fancier can prevent these problems, especially if the hedgehogs are young, by giving food that must be well chewed, and by adding a good calcium and vitamin supplement. Food that is too soft will not give the gums enough exercise. Older hedgehogs with tooth problems should be treated by a veterinarian. Symptoms in adult animals include foamy dribbling and foul breath. The lips may be red and swollen and the teeth, especially the back teeth, may be covered with a yellow deposit. The gums are swollen and deep red in color. The veterinarian will remove the deposits with appropriate dental instruments, and may treat with antibiotics or possibly vitamin C.

Spine loss: Do not be unduly alarmed if you find shed spines in your hedgehog's cage. In certain cases, especially in young hedgehogs, this is quite normal (see page 61). Do not forget that young hedgehogs go through a complete changeover of their spines. Of course, if the hedge-

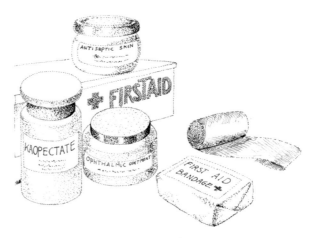

Despite meticulous care, a hedgehog may fall ill. A home medical kit will help you deal with minor emergencies.

hog suddenly gets bald patches that stay bald, you should be concerned. First of all, check to see if the animal has an infestation of mites, which perform their damaging work at the bases of the spines. If necessary, treat for mites and administer a good vitamin/mineral preparation with the food. Serious cases should be treated by a veterinarian.

Other disabilities: Various disabilities can arise as a result of lack of exercise in a confined space. Animals kept thus become fat and lazy, and may have difficulty in performing normal functions. In addition to a balanced diet, your hedgehogs must have space to exercise. This means a roomy exercise pen or area, plus the opportunity to run in the house and/or garden at regular, frequent intervals. Disabled hedgehogs must be referred to a veterinarian.

Animals confined in close quarters will also develop overgrown nails that can also make locomotion difficult. Hedgehogs must have the opportunity to climb and forage about, in order to

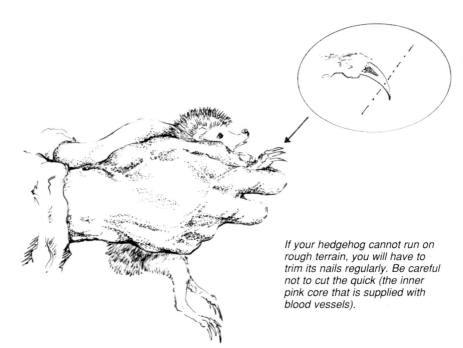

If your hedgehog cannot run on rough terrain, you will have to trim its nails regularly. Be careful not to cut the quick (the inner pink core that is supplied with blood vessels).

keep the nails short. With neglect, the outer nails will grow inward toward the sole of the foot, and this will cause problems if not immediately treated. You can help by placing a couple of flagstones in the run. The relatively rough surface of the stones will help abrade the nails to a normal length and maintain them in that condition.

You should clip the tips of the nails when necessary. Cut the nails as cleanly and naturally as possible, being careful not to clip them too short. Bird fanciers, who clip the nails of their parrots or parakeets, usually do it with the assistance of a second person; one holds the bird gently but firmly while the other clips the nails. An extra person would come in handy with hedgehogs as well. It is wise to wear leather gloves, and to have a moistened styptic pencil ready in case the nail is clipped too short and starts to bleed. Remember, when clipping nails, the second nail on the hind foot is naturally longer than the others.

Understanding Hedgehogs

As the various hedgehog species share many biological characteristics, a thorough description of one species will give a general picture of the entire genus. The best known of all hedgehogs is the European. Next is the African pygmy hedgehog, which, if you are planning to keep a hedgehog as a pet, is far and away the most likely choice.

The European Hedgehog (*Erinaceus europaeus*)

With two geographical races, western (*E. europaeus europaeus*, Linnaeus, 1758) and eastern (*E. europaeus roumanicus*, Barrett-Hamilton, 1900), the hedgehog is found in most parts of Europe and Asia. The eastern race occurs no further west than eastern Germany, whereas the western ranges over the whole of western Europe, including southern Scandinavia and northern Russia. The animal occurs up to an altitude of 6,560 feet (2,000 m). Neither race of European hedgehogs is found in the far north.

Physical Characteristics of the European Hedgehog

The body and limbs: The European hedgehog is a short, compact mammal with a pointed snout, short limbs, and a short tail. Adult hedgehogs have a length of 7 to 12 inches (18–30 cm). The thick tail is 0.5 to 2 inches (1.7–5 cm) long. The rear foot is 1.3 to 2 inches (3.4–5 cm) long, and the ear is 0.8 to 1.4 inches (2–3.5 cm) long. The animal weighs 21 to 28 ounces (600–800 g), and may rarely exceed 35 ounces (1 kg). There is little sexual dimorphism, although the male is generally somewhat larger than the female. European hedgehogs usually live for three to five years, but occasionally will reach the age of ten.

The coat and spines: The European hedgehog's most outstanding feature is, of course, its prickly coat. On its back there is not only a coat of normal hair, but also an armor of many sharp spines. These spines average 0.8 to 1.2 inches (2–3 cm) in length, and are about 1 mm thick. The spines are usually banded: gray at the base, then a yellowish-white zone, followed by a brownish-black zone, and ending in a light tip. Most of the spines are oriented posteriorly or dorsally (that is, pointing tailward or straight up when the animal is on the ground). Only those on the head and neck sometimes face in other directions. The legs, tail, and underside are covered with ordinary mammalian fur of a yellowish-brown color.

A seasonal molt or shedding of the spines does not occur. Old spines are, instead, replaced with new ones on a fairly continuous basis.

The snout is long and flexible, and the face is wrinkled, giving the animal an old and wise appearance. A set of black whiskers is situated on either side of the snout.

In many parts of Europe, including the Netherlands, Belgium, and Germany, folklore recognizes two kinds of hedgehogs: the "dog" hedgehog, with a pointed snout, and the "pig" hedgehog, with a shorter snout. The former is said to be a malicious beast from which your chickens in particular must be protected!

Of the two European races, *europaeus* and *roumanicus*, the former is supposed to have its snout shorter than its forehead, whereas the latter is the opposite. In my view, this is questionable, and I believe that the apparent differences in snouts have originated from the great flexibility of these structures and the vast variety of individuals.

In some parts of Europe, the hedgehog is only called by the name of the dog or pig hedgehog. The distinction of the two "sorts" is very old. Albertus Magnus (1193–1280) and Hilegard van Bingen (1090–1179), for example, mention having seen dog hedgehogs being used for food. Perhaps, as an old gypsy suggested to D. Mueller-Using, the dog hedgehog is nothing more than the inedible, skinny, spring hedgehog that, with a bountiful supply of food throughout the summer, will "metamorphose" into a plump pig hedgehog. (This suggestion has also been applied to the badger, another animal that hibernates and is thus thin in the spring and fat in the fall.)

The teeth and the alimentary canal: The shape of the 36 teeth reflect the hedgehog's omnivorous diet. The incisors are situated in the front of the upper and lower jaw, forming a set of tongs with which to grip the prey. The canines are not particularly well developed. The moderate length of the alimentary canal (seven times body length) is also related to the omnivorous diet. There is no appendix.

Diet of the European Hedgehog

The hedgehog's diet consists of more or less any animal matter it can find near or on the ground. Insects and their larvae, slugs, snails, and worms, lizards and snakes, frogs, moles, and young rabbits are all on the menu. Furthermore, they may plunder the nests of partridges or pheasants, occasionally even raiding the chicken house, although they are capable of opening only the smallest of eggs.

Vegetable food is rarely eaten by hedgehogs, though fruits, oily seeds, roots, and fungi are taken occasionally.

In *Natura,* January–April 1942, the Dutch zoologist, Dr. C. F. W. Doijer, reported that his seven captive hedgehogs preferred mainly meat, fat, milk, butter, cheese, fish, and fish bones. Vegetable foods taken included cooked potatoes, radishes, and oranges, as well as bread soaked in water or milk. Some would take jam or fruits (pears and berries). Offered a variety of foods, the animal based diets were preferred. (Today it is recognized that the feeding of high-fat diets to captive hedgehogs results in obesity, premature aging, and death.)

The hedgehog has a great appetite and drinks a lot of water. Dr. G. Roerig, a German zoologist, did some experiments in this connection. A healthy hedgehog that had received a meat (worms and insects) diet throughout the summer was given as many mealworms as it would eat from the beginning of October on. At the start of the test, the animal weighed 24.3 ounces (689 g). After ten days, it had eaten 66.3 ounces (1,880 g) of mealworms and it weighed not less than 40.7 ounces (1,155 g)! During the following ten days the hedgehog was fed with sparrows, of which it ate 45 with a weight of 51.6 ounces (1,462.4 g) (after deducting the feathers, which were not eaten). The hedgehog lost 2.3 ounces (63.5 g) of its body weight in this time, probably as a result of there being less fat in that particular diet. After this the animal ate no more

In the wild, the European hedgehog will forage for insects, larvae, snails, and worms. It will also hunt small reptiles and mammals.

and went into hibernation. At first it woke up occasionally, and ate a few mealworms. By December 10 it had eaten 4.3 ounces (120 g) of mealworms but weighed only 31.4 ounces (888.5 g), a loss of 7.2 ounces (203 g). Thereafter the hedgehog went into unbroken hibernation.

Feeding folklore: There are many folktales about the hedgehog's methods of getting food. The Roman writer Pliny (23–79 A.D.) told how hedgehogs spiked fruits on their spines in order to carry them home to feed the young. The Reverend J. F. Martinet also tells in his *Katechismus der natuur* (1778, 2, p. 122): "Another useful use of the spines. . . the hedgehog rolls under the fruit trees so that fruit is impaled on the spines and can thus be carried to his burrow" (freely translated). Although it is indeed true that hedgehogs have been seen and even photographed with fruit impaled on their spines, it is highly improbable that the animal does this with forethought. A more plausible explanation is that the animal rolls on its back to

help relieve the effects of biting skin parasites (especially ticks and mites) and may impale an apple or pear accidentally in the process.

Stories of hedgehogs taking milk from the teats of resting cows or goats can also be taken with a grain of salt. The hedgehog's mouth is much too small for this. However, one cannot discount the possibility that our spiky friend may lick on an udder should the occasion arise.

Habitat of the European Hedgehog

Hedgehogs prefer to live in areas where there is plenty of cover, such as woodland, hedges, thickets, tree roots, logs, and so on. In some areas, they are common in quiet parks and gardens in the towns and cities where they will take refuge in all kinds of nooks and crannies. They avoid very moist land, as well as grassland and other areas where cover is scarce.

The Senses

Research carried out by Dr. K. Herter, a German zoologist, offers a fair amount of knowledge about the European hedgehog's senses. The most important are those connected with its nocturnal lifestyle: smell, hearing, and touch.

Touch: The black whiskers are extremely sensitive tactile organs. If these are touched lightly, the hedgehog will pull itself together. If these whiskers are touched more heavily, it will roll itself up.

Smell: The hedgehog is extremely scent oriented. The mucous membranes lining the nasal passages are kept very moist, so that the animal can easily detect the direction of the smell. Every item it comes across in its wanderings is carefully sniffed and investigated with the snout. The sense of smell is very highly developed. Herter's hedgehogs reacted immediately when an unfamiliar smell or person came into their area.

Hearing: The fairly large ears are almost hidden below the coat. Notwithstanding, these organs are very sensitive, especially to squeaking, rustling, and smacking sounds. Hedgehogs are very alert, for example, to the sound of a camera shutter, and an electronic flash must take no longer than 0.01 seconds if you want to get the head clearly in the picture!

Sight: Hedgehogs generally show interest in moving objects, but are less interested in the colors and shapes of things. Tests have shown that hedgehogs can distinguish many objects, if you are able to hold their attention. Herter gave his hedgehogs this problem: Of a number of sliding doors, one must be pushed open to get a reward. Of the three doors, only pushing the one on the right resulted in a reward, whereas pushing other doors resulted in punishment. In the first ten tests, the left was chosen once, the middle nil, the right six times. In the second series of ten tests, the left and middle doors were chosen nil, and the right ten

times; in the third series, the results were respectively one, nil, and nine.

A similar test was carried out for recognition of light and dark, and for various colors. With light and dark, for example, there were two white doors and one black door. The animal was rewarded for opening the black door, and punished for opening the white doors. After 550 tests, it had been trained to 80 percent accuracy in a 50-test series. When one door was blue and the other two yellow, the same result was reached after only 200 tests.

Once the animals were trained to recognize one color, the color was changed. They would choose the other color, not the yellow, even with a lighter color. This shows that the hedgehogs had learned that yellow was the punishment color. This proves again the axiom that animals learn more quickly in relation to what is important to them in nature, than things that are less important.

Hibernation

During the cold months of November through March, when food is scarce, the European hedgehog goes into hibernation. It chooses a hollow in the ground and covers itself with leaves and other ground litter. At first, the sleep is not too deep and may be occasionally interrupted (I have seen hedgehogs in England and the Netherlands walking about in the snow). Later the hedgehog goes into a deep hibernation, with its accompanying drop in body temperature and loss of consciousness. In this state, the animal does not react to sounds and is curled up into a tight ball, completely surrounded by its spines (which is not the case with normal sleep).

Hibernation begins when the nest temperature drops to 59.5° to 63.5°F (15°–17.5°C), when the outside temperature is about 50.5°F (10.5°C).

With the nest temperature at 58.5°F to 63.5°F (14.5–17.5°C), the hedgehog is still half-awake. Only when the temperature drops below 58.5°F (14.5°C) does the proper hibernation begin. Body temperature falls to less than 57.5°F (14.2°C). At nest temperatures between 58.5° and 42.5°F (14.5°–5.6°C), the hibernating hedgehog's body temperature will remain one degree higher. When the temperature drops below 42.5°F (5.6°C), the hedgehog produces just enough body warmth to maintain it at 42.9°F (6.5°C). If the temperature stays below 42.5°F (5.6°C) for too long, however, the hedgehog gets warmer and its body temperature soon reaches its normal active temperature of 95.5°F (34.5°C), at which point it wakes up.

The animal tries to choose its nesting place to maintain an even temperature. Prolonged cold will eventually waken it, but heat will do the trick much more quickly. You can get a hibernating captive hedgehog to wake up in two to five hours by raising its nest temperature to 63.5° to 75.3°F (17.5°–24.5°C).

Naturally, the low body temperature of hibernation means that little energy is used. To awaken, the hedgehog requires a lot of energy to raise its temperature to the normal working range. This rise in temperature starts well before the animal awakes. Breathing and heart rate become faster and stronger. The warmth is produced by immense muscle activity, which is visible as a heavy quivering in the waking animal. This is basically the same as shivering in humans.

Aspects of Behavior

In contrast with most nocturnal animals, the hedgehog is quite noisy. It can easily be heard snuffling in its search for food, and, after it drinks, you can often hear it coughing and sneezing. When in danger, it screams loudly. Anger, pain, and fear are expressed with a loud "ke-ke-ke."

If necessary, hedgehogs can swim quite well for long periods. They do not like the water, however, and will seek out dry land again as fast as possible.

As hedgehogs are mainly solitary, only single specimens are usually seen. Occasionally, however, a male and female may be seen together outside the breeding season, sometimes even sharing a nest. Several nests may be found in a small area.

Hedgehogs are generally sedentary and spend most of their time in a single area, always retiring to the same nest. Sometimes the hedgehog makes a burrow with two entrances. The nest material, mainly foliage, is carried in the mouth.

Foraging: When foraging for food, the hedgehog scratches and probes in the ground litter with its feet and snout, leaving its characteristic visiting cards, the typical, pointed, sausage-like droppings.

Hedgehogs are occasionally active during the day but do not usually forage then, except perhaps after heavy rain, when slugs and snails abound. Captive specimens peak activity usually occurs between 6 to 8:30 P.M., 12:30 to 2:30 A.M., and 4 to 5:30 A.M. Wild hedgehogs seem to be active at similar times, but this has not yet been proved.

Rolling behavior: At the approach of danger, or when sleeping or hibernating, the European hedgehog will roll itself into a tight ball. It also sleeps rolled up, but there is an easily distinguishable difference between the normal resting ball, and the ball of hibernation or fright. In the first case, the animal is only partly rolled up and breathing deeply, whereas the hibernating or frightened animal is completely rolled up with the spines protecting all sides. In the latter case breathing is very slow, shallow, and irregular.

European hedgehogs are frequently found in parks and gardens where there is plenty of cover.

The spines are usually an excellent defense against predators. Most dogs will avoid the hedgehog because of its spines, but should a wily dog find a hedgehog close to a pond or stream, it may try roll its prey into the water. In order to swim, the hedgehog will have to unroll and expose its vulnerable underside to the dog, who can then make a quick killing. Foxes are said to behave in a similar manner. Foxes will also roll the hedgehog over so that it lays on its back, and then will urinate into the cavity into which the hedgehog withdraws its head and limbs. The acrid, strong smelling urine of the fox is said to make the hedgehog unroll.

J. Ritzema Bos told of often seeing hedgehogs rolling into a ball and dropping from heights, such as from walls or lofts, and landing uninjured. Dr. Ritzema Bos states that these animals are able to fall easily from heights of 19 feet (5.8m) without injury.

Reproduction

In the breeding season, European hedgehogs follow each other about and fight a lot. Emitting strange snorting and whistling noises, the rivals charge each other with their head spines directed forward. However, these skirmishes rarely draw blood. Because it is difficult to determine the sexes of hedgehogs, it may be difficult to determine if these battles involve only males (as would normally be assumed), or both males and females.

The gestation period is five to six weeks, and the female gives birth to three to seven young, sometimes more. There may be one or two litters during the breeding season, which lasts from late March to July. The young are born from May to August, and come into the world blind and helpless. The mother looks after them and protects them fiercely against intruders, up to and including humans. If the nest is disturbed, she will carry the young away in her mouth.

The offspring: The newborn babies are about as big as your little finger, 3 to 4.5 inches (7.5–11.4 cm). They already have soft, white spines about 3 mm long. About 36 to 60 hours after birth, colored spines start to appear between the already lengthened white ones. After 14 days, a third set of spines appears and the first and second sets of juvenile spines fall out. The juvenile spines are situated in regular rows, but not the adult spines, which have a more random distribution. After a week, the spines can be erected, and after 11 days the young start trying to roll up, but they do not succeed completely until after a few days of practice.

The hairs on the underside of the body appear after 16 days, whereas the whiskers on the snout do not appear until 60 to 120 days after birth. The eyes, closed at birth, open at 14 days, and about 14 days later, at the age of a month, the young begin to leave the nest with their mother. By that time they are able to regulate their body temperature. The mother takes them foraging for food, and the young stay close to her. If one of the babies should lose contact with the troop, it lets out a few cries to inform the mother of its whereabouts and she will round it up. After four weeks the teeth are well developed, and the young nurse less and less, ceasing completely after about six weeks.

At their first hibernation the juveniles are still very young, about four months old, and in very cold weather some of the weaker ones may die.

A hedgehog is mature at one year of age and lives for three to ten years.

European Hedgehogs and People

It is well known that farmers and grain merchants liked to keep hedgehogs because they believed them to be adept mouse catchers. Though in old illustrations one often sees a hedgehog with a mouse in its jaws, and Dr. J. Ritzema Bos, writing in *Tijdschrift over plantenziekten* (*Plant Disease Journal*), September, 1918, extolled the hedgehog's prowess as a mouser, there seems to be little evidence that this is true.

It is also common knowledge that hedgehogs overpower snakes, such as the European grass snake (*Natrix natrix*) or the venomous adder (*Vipera berus*). In the case of the latter species the hedgehog is very careful, in spite of the fact that scientific tests have shown the hedgehog to be resistant to many poisons, including adder venom. It is 2,000 times less sensitive to tetanus toxin than a human being, and 40 times less sensitive to adder venom than a guinea pig.

Despite its caution, the hedgehog gives no ground to the adder. Holding its head down and keeping low, it offers only its spines for the reptile to strike at. Sometimes it takes a long time, maybe more than an hour, for the hedgehog to overpower its victim and dispatch it with a bite through the spinal column.

The hedgehog's gift of immunity to adder venom has been exploited by scientists using its blood to make antivenin. To date, however, experiments in this field have not been successful.

This prickly friend is known at least as well as the mole by both young and old in Europe, and most people have an affection for it. Some animal lovers like to watch the hedgehog slurping up the dish of milk they have offered, whereas others erroneously regard it as an insurance against mice.

People's interest in hedgehogs has not always been beneficial for the animals. In many areas they are cooked and eaten. During World War I, for example, in the eastern Netherlands many hedgehogs found their way into cooking pots. Similar stories were told by French workers

A female European hedgehog (Erinaceus europaeus europaeus) *and her young. The mother is about to capture a succulent beetle.*

who were brought to work in Germany during World War II. In earlier times people found curative uses for the fat, blood, and viscera of the hedgehog, while the Romans used its spiny skin to card wool.

Hedgehogs can be generally regarded as harmless animals, and are protected fauna in most countries. They can, perhaps, do a little damage in the forestry industry by grubbing out newly planted seeds or saplings in their search for insects, but this is more than made up for by the vast amounts of invertebrate pests they eat.

The African Pygmy Hedgehog

The main subject of this book, the African pygmy hedgehog (*Erinaceus* or *Atelerix albiventris*), is described in various zoological books or field guides as the white-bellied, four-toed, or East African hedgehog. These names already suggest differences from the European hedgehog, though there are also many similarities.

Physical Characteristics of the African Pygmy Hedgehog

The body and limbs: The most outstanding difference, of course, is in the size of the animal: the African pygmy hedgehog is about 6 inches (15 cm) long, with spines ½ to 1 inch (1.5–2.5 cm) in length. The average weight of a full grown specimen is 18 to 25 ounces (500–700 g). The forefeet have five toes, and the rear feet only four. The female has ten teats. The ears are shorter than the head spines, round in shape, and finely haired.

The coat and spines: The head has a spine-free zone in the center of the crown. The back is furnished with a thick coat of grooved spines. These are white or "salt and pepper" in color, with a broad, dark, blackish-brown band, giving an overall impression of black and white stippling. The snout is brownish, whereas the forehead, cheeks, underside, and legs are white. There are, however, color variations including blacks, whites, snowflakes, and creams.

Diet of the
African Pygmy Hedgehog

Natural food items include worms, insects, slugs, snails, crustaceans, frogs, lizards, snakes, eggs, nestling birds, small mammals, carrion, fruits and seeds (including peanuts), fungi, and roots. Due to the great variety of acceptable foods, it is not often necessary for the hedgehog to forage over great distances, but intruders will always be driven out of its territory.

An African pygmy hedgehog eats an average of one third of its own body weight each night. Small prey animals are simply bitten to death; with snakes the back is broken first. It is thought that this species is also (at least relatively) immune to snakebite. It has also been found that insecticides and other agricultural chemicals often have little or no immediate effect on them!

Habitat of the
African Pygmy Hedgehog

The African pygmy hedgehog occurs across a large tract of dry land from western Africa to southern Somalia and Tanzania. It is an animal of the savanna, a terrain of grassland interspersed with thick brush and occasional stands of trees. African pygmy hedgehogs are also often common in settled areas, especially in parks and gardens. I have also found this animal in the mountains at altitudes of 6,560 feet (2,000 m).

The Senses

This species also has excellent olfactory and auditory powers. Experiments have shown that hedgehogs can smell prey that is up to 2 inches (5 cm) below the ground (buried or burrowed). The sight of the African pygmy hedgehog is better than that of its European cousin, but its color recognition is poorly developed.

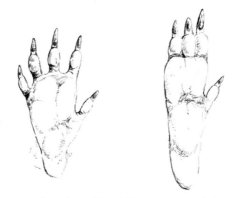

The front feet of the African pygmy hedgehog has five toes (left); the rear feet have only four toes (right).

Aspects of Behavior

The territory of a single animal has a radius of 220 to 330 yards (200 to 300 m) around its burrow. This may be enlarged during food shortages. During the day, the animal sleeps in its burrow, which may be in a termite mound or in the ground under a pile of rocks. I have also found hedgehogs in rock crevices, or under thick ground litter in a hollow, more or less covered with vegetation. Three times I have found one under the wooden foundations of a barn or a native house, and twice in a hollow against the foundations of an aircraft hangar.

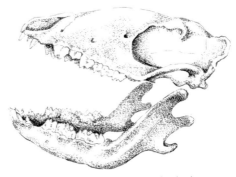

The teeth of the African pygmy hedgehog are suited to its omnivorous diet.

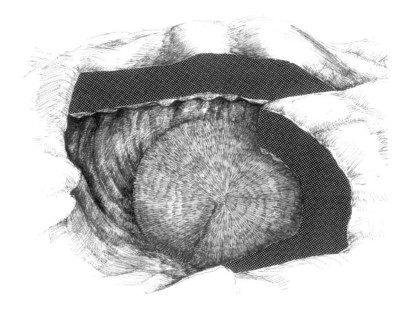

The African pygmy hedgehog goes into aestivation during the dry season. It sleeps in its underground burrow, which is more or less covered with vegetation.

Aestivation: During the course of my study of this species (long before it became a popular pet animal), I discovered that it aestivated during the dry season when food was scarce. During this time, the animal lives off its fat reserves, much as does the hibernating European hedgehog (see page 58).

Foraging: The African pygmy hedgehog becomes active at dusk and will forage casually for most of the night. If necessary, however, it can put on a burst of speed with its short limbs in order to seek out a safe hideaway. It is also an adept swimmer, should the need arise.

After catching and subduing its prey, it licks its snout, sometimes wetting it with saliva. If disturbed while foraging, the hedgehog rolls itself up and begins to sniff and growl, although the African pygmy hedgehogs are generally less aggressive and nervous than the European species.

Self-anointing: If an African pygmy hedgehog should come across unfamiliar smelling or tasting materials or objects, they are licked and chewed, during which copious quantities of saliva are produced. Using its tongue, the hedgehog spreads the resulting foam over its spines. Similar behavior can sometimes be observed when hedgehogs meet, especially during the breeding season.

Vocalizations: The normal sounds of the African pygmy hedgehog are high chirping notes made with the mouth closed. These are often accompanied by snuffling noises when the animal is disturbed. I have heard the latter noise frequently in the pet shop when the animals are handled by strangers or taken to strange surroundings.

In the wild, these animals are also far from peaceful. If an intruder should turn up in the territory of another, the latter will show its displeasure with loud snorting and hissing noises that increase in frequency and volume as its agitation increases.

These noises could be compared to those made by a nervous, excited, or tortured cat. Should the irritation continue, the next stage is a series of loud growling noises, which my grand-

It is thought that the African pygmy hedgehog is virtually immune to snake venom.
Here, a viper and a hedgehog are about to attack each other.

Self-anointing: Like other hedgehogs, the African pygmy will spread copious amounts of
saliva over its spines from time to time. It is possible that this habit may aid in pest control.

When unrolling, the head of the African pygmy hedgehog is raised and the spinal column is straightened by muscles attached to the skull, neck, vertebrae and tail.

daughter once likened to the spluttering of a small motor. If really angry, or fighting, the animals twitter loudly and constantly. When in pain or in mortal danger, they can scream loudly.

Rolling behavior: In the wild, African pygmy hedgehogs have various natural enemies. The most important are great eagle owls (*Bubo lacteus*), honey badgers, jackals, and wild dogs. As soon as real danger is present, the hedgehog rolls itself into a protective, prickly ball.

Reproduction

In courtship, the male serenades the female with continuous twittering, growling, and snorting noises while running around her in circles. At first the female tries to ignore him, or may react with hisses and snorts of her own. She may run away or curl up. But the suitor is persistent, and his proposed mate eventually accedes to his desires.

During mating, the female flattens out her spines and stretches out her rear limbs. With his extra long penis, the male finds little difficulty in copulating. After copulation, the vagina becomes closed with a *seminal plug*.

The gestation period is 30 to 40 days. Birth in the wild takes place in a subterranean chamber lined with bedding material. Two to ten young may be born, with an average of five in the litter. The mother licks the young to clean and dry them as soon as they are born. She also eats the afterbirth. Once this has been done, the mother picks up the young in her mouth and guides them to her teats.

The offspring: At birth, the tiny, blind young weigh about 0.43 to 0.63 ounces (12–18 g). Only the start of tiny, soft, white spines are present on the almost naked skin. After two or three days, a few black spines start to grow between the white ones. The eyes open after 8 to 18 days.

The babies grow quickly, and are able to roll themselves into a ball in a week or two. After 30 to 35 days, the young possess permanent spines, and lose the white ones.

Then the mother starts taking her babies on short outings. They learn to

An African pygmy hedgehog in the process of unrolling comes face to face with a giant scorpion.

Should the need arise, the African pygmy hedgehog can take to the water to flee from danger.

A rare two-tone African pygmy hedgehog.

This white hedgehog is not an albino. It is the result of a spontaneous mutation.

A white bellied or pruners African pygmy hedgehog.

A pure Algerian hedgehog.

forage for food, but continue to nurse for about 10 more days. After one and a half to two months, the youngsters are independent and leave the mother. They become sexually mature at about one year of age.

Other Hedgehog Species

The Somali hedgehog (*Erinaceus* or *Atelerix sclateri*) is very similar to the African pygmy hedgehog, but has five toes on the rear foot. The underside is not white, but is usually brown or mainly brown in color. In spite of these obvious differences some zoologists believe this animal to be not even a subspecies, but merely a variety of *E. albiventris*. It occurs well into northern Somalia, but its general range overlaps that of *E. albiventris*.

The South African hedgehog (*Erinaceus* or *Atelerix frontalis*) is an even smaller species. Fully grown specimens weigh 9 to 21 ounces (260 to 600 g). They have five digits on each foot. In its native land this animal serves as both a well loved pet and as a food item, but the chances of it turning up outside that country are pretty remote. The animal was declared to be scarce by the South African zoologist Dr. J. Meesters in 1975, and is now listed, deservedly, I believe, on Appendix 2 of the CITES list.

This species has white spines with broad, brown bands. The snout and cheeks are dark brown, and there is a conspicuous white band on the forehead. Most of the underside is white, and the feet, along with the underside of the tail, are gray to dark brown, occasionally with white flecks. Albinos are regularly reported.

Apart from South Africa, they occur in northern and southwestern Angola, western and eastern Botswana, Zimbabwe, southern Zambia, southern Malawi, and central Mozambique. They require an environment with a minimum of 11.8 inches (300 mm) of rain per annum. The natural habitat consists of savanna, open grassland, and vegetated *kopjes* (an Afrikaans word for high, isolated hillocks).

One of the most obvious behavioral differences between this and the two preceding species is that the South African hedgehog does not make a permanent home, and seeks out a fresh refuge every morning after a night of foraging. The animal usually conceals itself in thick, high grass, beneath rocks, or in ground litter. The animals hibernate during the coldest periods of the southern winter (May to August).

Reproductive behavior is similar to that of the preceding species. The gestation period is about 40 days, and the young are born from October to March. The four to nine young weigh 0.32 to 0.43 ounces (9–12 g) at birth.

The vagrant or Algerian hedgehog (*Erinaceus* or *Atelerix algirus*) is a somewhat larger African species. This animal stands conspicuously high on its limbs, and has larger ears. The spines are white with narrow darker bands. The head and legs are brown, and the underside may be white or brown.

Algerian hedgehogs can be found from Morocco to western Libya with the exception of the drier desert areas, also occurring on Fuerteventura, Gran Canaria, and Tenerife in the Canary Islands, and the warmer parts of Europe, including eastern Spain, southern France, and the Balearic Islands. The animal is often seen in parks and gardens, even bringing youngsters to nearby house doors in search of free handouts.

This species will hibernate when temperatures drop sufficiently low. The gestation period is 35 to 48 days and three to seven young per litter are born. There are often two litters per season.

The big- or long-eared hedgehog
(*Hemiechinus auritus*), is an interesting species that has a very wide natural range. You will see by its scientific name, that this species is in another genus, which also has another, lesser known species, *H. dauuricus.*

H. auritus has a slender build and stands high on its limbs. Total length is 6–11 inches (15–28 cm), the tail accounting for 0.4–2.25 inches (1–5.5 cm) of that. Its weight is 14–18 ounces (400–500 g). The snout is sharply pointed, and this, together with the large, pointed ears, which reach far out of the spiny coat (probably a desert adaptation for heat radiation), gives this species a striking appearance.

The spines are banded in white and brown. They are grooved and feel rough to the touch. On the back, most of the cream-colored spines are about 0.6 inches (1.5 cm) long. The face is white, or brownish; the ears, the legs, and the tail are white; the underside is light brown to white; and the feet are gray-brown. The female has ten teats.

The long-eared hedgehog is found from northern Libya, through Egypt and southwestern Asia, to India and Mongolia. I have found various specimens along the Nile southward as far as Fayum, and they also are found on Cyprus. The habitat of this species is largely semidesert and arid steppe. In Egypt it occurs sporadically in poorly vegetated areas, but I have also found them in parks and gardens. In some regions they are common around human habitations.

Most of the long-eared hedgehogs I studied in Africa seldom or never made their own nest or burrow, but preferred to use existing burrows or hollows. However, it is interesting to note that this same species in other areas may dig out a burrow, sometimes as much as 3.3 feet (1 m) deep, and use it as a permanent home. The burrows in the Rajasthan Desert of India, some of

The long-eared desert hedgehog (Hemiechinus auritus) is found from northern Lybia, through Egypt and southwestern Asia, to India and Mongolia.

which can be 4.9 feet (1.5 m) long, are made only under small, thick shrubs, and have a single entrance and exit. Only a single animal lives in such a burrow, but the female will make a wider nesting chamber to accommodate her young. There is normally only one litter per season.

Members of the genus *Hemiechinus* are nocturnal and territorial. According to E. P. Walker, *H. auritus* hibernates for up to three and a half months in the Punjab region of northern India. In the mountains of Pakistan the hibernation lasts from October to March, whereas in warmer areas there may be no hibernation at all, but rather irregular aestivation brought on by scarcity of food.

As with other hedgehog species, the preferred food consists of insects and other invertebrates, small vertebrates, eggs, berries and other fruits, seeds and roots, and carrion. This species is quite resistant to hunger and thirst. Self-anointing behavior occurs, just as with *Erinaceus* species.

My tip: The lifestyle of the long-eared hedgehog shows it to be a solitary animal, and in captivity at least, it has been reported to be antisocial to the point of cannibalism. My own expe-

71

rience does not support this contention, and I have found that as long as these hedgehogs have adequate food and water, they will avoid each other and live peacefully, even in captivity.

The other species in the genus, *H. dauuricus*, occurs in the eastern Gobi Desert region, from Lake Baikal to northern China.

The desert hedgehog
(*Paraechinus aethiopicus*), is the last African species. This animal is shorter, and has rounder ears than its larger cousin, the long-eared hedgehog. A spineless zone runs over the crown. Total length is 5.5 to 10.5 inches (14–27 cm), and the tail is only 0.4 to 1.6 inches (1–4 cm) long. Males can sometimes weigh as much as 15.4 ounces (435 g), lactating females up to 11 ounces (310 g). The underside is thickly covered with soft fur, which may be blotched dark brown and white, or tinted with various other colors. The spines on the back average 1.1 inches (2.7 cm), and are light colored with two dark bands. The pointed snout and relatively short ears are dark brown, the forehead and the flanks are white, and the feet and tail are dark brown. There are variations of this general color scheme, and I have seen individuals that were wholly dark brown, and others that were almost wholly white except for the feet and tail. The female has ten teats.

This species lives in desert and arid terrains of northern Africa, south to Timbuktu (Mali), Air (Niger), Sennar (Sudan), northern Ethiopia, and northern Somalia. They also occur in the Arabian Peninsula. Four subspecies are generally recognized. All are mainly terrestrial and nocturnal. Walker said that ". . . in the Salloum village area of Egypt, the desert hedgehog is reported to rest in the cliffs during the day, and to forage on the coastal plain at night."

This animal, which keeps a store of food in its burrow, lives mainly on insects. It also takes small vertebrates, the eggs of ground-nesting birds, and even scorpions! The female enlarges her permanent nest hollow when preparing to give birth, or makes a special nest at a concealed site above the ground. There is a single litter per year, consisting of one to four and sometimes up to six babies.

Immediately after birth, the mother licks the underside of her newborns to activate the digestive and urinary systems. She will ingest the droppings and urine while cleaning up. Should danger approach, the mother will become very aggressive, and will attack the intruder with her head spines directed forward while letting out furious screaming noises.

The young suckle for about two months and, at about forty days of age, begin to take solid food, which the mother brings to the nest. At birth the young weigh about ⅓ ounce (8–9 g), after four weeks about 2 ounces (55–57 g), at six weeks about 3 ounces (82–85 g), and after ten weeks about 5.7 ounces (160 g). At around two months of age, they are about half the size of their mother.

Two other species in the *Paraechinus* genus are Brandt's hedgehog (*P. hypomelas*) and the Indian hedgehog (*P. micropus*). Brandt's hedgehog is found around the Aral Sea, southwest to Pakistan and northern India, and southwest to southern Iran and the southern Arabian Peninsula. The Indian hedgehog is found mainly in Pakistan and the western parts of India, its range overlapping that of the long-eared hedgehog.

When stressed or frightened, or when pursuing prey (such as a toad), *P. micropus* can run at a speed of 1.9 miles (3 km) per hour, whereas it normally travels at 0.68 miles (1.09 km) per hour. This species also stores food in its burrow for future use, though it is generally accepted that it does not take any plant food. *P. hypomelas*, however, eats fruit, insects, and small vertebrates.

In the wild, these hedgehogs will go into aestivation if food becomes scarce. They must therefore eat as much as possible during the more plentiful times to ensure that they always have adequate fat reserves to bring them through a lean period.

Hedgehog Characteristics in General

The most outstanding feature of a hedgehog is its coat of spines, which takes up as much as 35 percent of its total body weight. These spines augment the normal mammalian fur cover and are, in fact, modified hairs. It is easy to see that these spines are not a particularly good insulation, and a lot of heat must be lost through them in the colder weather.

The animal therefore strives, during the warmer parts of the year, to eat enough food to provide it with a thick layer of fat. It then retires to a burrow, or hollow, often under a layer of earth or leaves, to fall into the deep sleep of hibernation. In this state, the respiratory rate and pulse are dramatically reduced to conserve energy (see page 8).

Rolling

Another typical hedgehog characteristic is the presence of strong *orbicularis* muscles situated under the skin along the line where the spines and the hair meet. To roll up, the muscles—which are attached to the skull and the tail—contract and shorten the outer (lateral) edge of the spiny part of the skin. The hedgehog pulls in its belly, head and limbs so that they are surrounded by the muscular, spiny skin, forming an almost impenetrable ball. When unrolling, the head is brought up (extended) and the spinal column straightened by the spinal extensor muscles which are attached to the skull, spinal column, and tail.

Using these special muscles, the hedgehog, at the first sign of danger, "rolls" itself up, presenting a daunting, prickly ball to the would-be assailant. The orbicularis is attached to very mobile connective tissue, and has a good blood supply. It divides into five branches near the head, making it possible for the hedgehog to erect the spines on its forehead and direct them forward (like a visor) when lesser dangers threaten. Under normal circumstances, including danger, the spines all point in the same direction. But if great danger threatens, the hedgehog can make the spines crisscross to the right and left. The animal is also able to creep through narrow openings. In other words, it can make its body flatter or taller.

Self-anointing

Once you have kept a pet hedgehog for a while, you will undoubtedly notice that your little friend seems to be irresistibly attracted to certain objects that are quite inedible, but perhaps have an agreeable scent.

The most outstanding characteristic of all hedgehog species is the spiny coat, which constitutes as much as 35 percent of the body's weight.

(Understandably, these odors may often be agreeable only to the hedgehog!) Such items may include leather shoes, bags, and gloves (leather furniture will drive some hedgehogs "nuts"), tobacco (a neglected ashtray will always be examined), cameras, typewriters (perhaps the smell of the oil?), and plants with volatile oils.

As well as sniffing and chewing at objects, the hedgehog seems to take in the scent. The snout is held in the air and the upper lip is pulled up while the animal makes licking and chewing movements, as if trying to absorb the scent. At the same time it salivates profusely, producing a foam that, with long strokes of the tongue, is spread over the spines of the neck and back, as well as on the hair along the flanks. This is known as *self-anointing*.

During anointing, the spines may become somewhat entangled. Sometimes the animal is so intensively busy with this behavior, reaching ever further over its back, that it falls over! No problem, for lying on its back, it will continue to anoint itself. When it is satisfied with its work, the animal shakes itself thoroughly, so that its spines are again brought back into alignment.

Jacobson's Organ

Why do hedgehogs anoint themselves with saliva when exposed to particular scents or tastes? They possess a special olfactory organ called the *Jacobson's organ*. This structure is found not only in hedgehogs, but in other mammals, such as cats and some hoofed animals, as well as in the higher primates.

Jacobson's organ is a tubular sac set in the palate, near the base of the nostril. Lined with olfactory sensory cells, the organ is efficient at processing a combination of scent and taste. Secretions from mucous glands keep the interior of the organ clean and ready

for action. The resulting salivary secretions are the basis for self-anointing. It is not known why the hedgehog anoints only itself, and not its surroundings.

Hibernation and Aestivation

I have already discussed hibernation in some detail (see page 8), and have noted that other forms of specialized sleeping, such as aestivation, which I have studied personally, are similar to hibernation. A few further observations here will not be amiss, though the average keeper of African pygmy hedgehogs will be confronted seldom or never with a hibernation or aestivation situation.

A look at the seasonal restraints facing the European hedgehog will clearly show why hibernation is necessary; its staple insect diet is almost totally absent during the winter months. Hibernation is thus an essential phase in the animal's life if it is to survive. Moreover, the coat of spines would be but poor protection during protracted cold times, and hibernation is really the only way out.

Metabolism is dramatically reduced during hibernation, and providing the animal finds itself a protective burrow and goes to sleep with adequate fat reserves, it should wake up fit and healthy the following spring. Of course, a great deal of its fat reserves will have been used up, and the animal will emerge somewhat slimmer than it was a few months earlier. Average loss during this time is 20 to 25 percent of the body weight.

Hedgehogs that live in warm, dry regions will aestivate when circumstances (drought, high temperatures) require it. However, it has become clear that hibernation or aestivation is not essential to hedgehogs that continue to receive adequate food and are not subjected to temperature extremes.

Sometimes a hedgehog will, for no explicable reason, eat more than it should and become overweight. It will become sleepy and lethargic, and may even sleep for a few days, before it again becomes active. As long as it is kept to a good feeding regime, such behavior is nothing to worry about. In the wild, hibernating hedgehogs frequently awaken before the beginning of spring. There can be various reasons for this: a long period of exceptionally cold weather, sudden warmth, hunger, or disturbance by human or animal life.

The actual process of waking up itself is a strain on the heart and blood circulation, as the hedgehog's cold body has to be quickly raised to full operating temperature. In the European hedgehog, for example, I have established that the heart beats 320 times per minute when the temperature is being raised, as opposed to 180 to 220 beats under normal circumstances.

Sometimes the strain of awakening will cause the animal to collapse, and it may even appear to be dying. The animal can lay in a sort of coma for up to five minutes, a worrying time for the novice hedgehog fancier! It should not be placed in a warm spot, however, at least not above 59°F (15°C).

Once the animal is fully awake, you must see that it has immediate access to food and water, otherwise there is a chance that it will die of exhaustion. European hedgehog lovers are advised to feed wild hedgehogs that have awakened before May. You can save their lives by doing this!

The same goes for animals that appear to be almost dead and for some reason or another have used up nearly all of their reserves and have not awakened in time. If such animals are not given help by humans, they will surely die.

Studies have shown that hedgehogs newly emerged from hibernation are usually "back to normal" in a few

A well-developed olfactory sense is probably the hedgehog's most important aid in locating its prey.

days and remember their surroundings. It was long thought that hedgehogs had to virtually "start over again" with regard to orienting themselves, but the German biologist Helga Fritzsche reported that her tame male hedgehog immediately recognized her, perhaps by her voice, after spending summer and winter free in a park. As she spoke to him from her terrace in the evening, he immediately stopped, listening and sniffing, then came a few steps closer. All other wild hedgehogs would have shown fear and probably rolled into a ball!

The Food of Wild Hedgehogs

A look at all of the various hedgehog species reveals an extremely varied menu. Insects, worms, snails, and the nestlings of mice and other small mammals stand high on the list. But small crabs, lizards, snakes, eggs and young of ground-nesting birds, carrion, various fruits, peanuts, many different seeds, fungi, roots, small fish, frogs, and even scorpions are also eaten when the opportunity arises.

Of course, not all hedgehogs will eat all of what is listed, or in any great amount. Vegetables, for example, may be eaten only occasionally.

Stories and legends are widespread that hedgehogs catch mice (see page 61). However, while the

Hedgehogs are solitary animals— except during the breeding season.

hedgehog is not exactly a slow animal, it is not quick enough to catch a mouse. Mice are much more agile, as are voles (*Microtinae* or *Arvicolinae*). Do not believe gardening books that may say the opposite! Hedgehogs can indeed excavate well, but voles are much too fast for them! I have seen the European hedgehog eat mice left by our cat and, although they take their time, they consume the entire carcass, including the fur and bones.

The Family

If you believe the popular children's stories (see Preface), hedgehogs live in happy families of parents and their offspring. Nothing is further from the truth! Outside of the breeding season, females as well as males are totally solitary, though sometimes a female will be accompanied by her young for an extended period. After fertilizing a female, the male usually has no further interest in his "wife," and will probably never see his "children." Young hedgehogs develop very quickly and are soon independent The only family behavior demonstrated is when the mother takes her procession of little ones on foraging expeditions through a park or gardens. This maternal behavior is exhibited by both the European and the African pygmy hedgehog.

Mother hedgehogs usually will have nothing to do with the young of others. In captivity, however, a female will occasionally accept a foster child if it is presented properly. One must place the foster child with the rest of the litter when the mother is not present, so that it can assume the scent of her own young. This can be a long and difficult process. A rejected youngster will not be allowed to suckle, though the mother may permit it to remain in the nest and not harm it in any other way.

Reproduction

Breeding: The breeding season really begins during the period of hibernation in those species that do so. Only when the females are fertilized, have given birth, and have raised their young, can it be said that the breeding season is over.

During the long breeding season, males are very aggressive when seeking a female, and rivals are savagely driven off. Sometimes competing males will try to shove each other with their spines, or may even try to bite the non-spiny parts (shoulders, belly, and flanks) of their adversaries. The shoulders are particularly vulnerable and are frequently injured. Unfortunately many animals die, not so much from the wounds directly, but from the infections that often follow. The weaker hedgehog has two ways of avoiding further conflict with the stronger: running away or rolling into a ball and waiting for the aggressor to leave.

When a male approaches a female, she often emits puffing sounds of protest, but this does not deter him, and he pursues her, making twittering, growling, and puffing noises. For her part the female will begin to hiss and puff and continue to run, but the male's persistence eventually wins out! It is amusing to watch what I like to call "boxing" with the head while yelping. The African pygmy hedgehog is an expert in this behavior!

During mating, the female lays her spines flat against her body and stretches out her hind limbs. After a successful copulation, the vagina of the female African pygmy hedgehog becomes filled and obstructed by a *seminal plug* that inhibits further mating, and, in any event, gravid females will not allow further copulation.

Gestation and Birth: The gestation period of the African pygmy hedgehog is 30 to 40 days. Birth takes place in a nursery chamber, which is newly lined with leaves, moss, grass, and similar bedding materials. Litter size ranges from two to ten, five being average. The babies are licked carefully by the mother hedgehog as soon as they are born, and she also eats the afterbirth. Then she takes the young in her mouth and places them on her teats to suckle.

Sometimes a male may nest with his pregnant wife, but if he should come around after the young are born, he is quickly chased away!

Newborn African pygmy hedgehogs are blind, and weigh 0.4 to 0.7 ounces (12–18 g). They are initially spineless, but these appear two or three days after birth. Newborn European hedgehogs do have spines, but they cannot hurt the mother, as the tips are still embedded in the skin. The spines grow very quickly. After 24 hours, about one third of their length is visible.

The mother licks her newborn young strongly with her warm tongue, in order to promote respiration and blood circulation. Although the nest is warmly lined, for the first few days the young lie close to their mother, who herself lies on her side.

Though she possesses ten teats, a mother may have difficulties with large litters. Weaker youngsters are pushed away by their stronger siblings and will lag in their development. Even if they do not starve to death, they will still be weak and will not be likely to survive for long.

However, one cannot say that hedgehogs do not make good mothers;

quite the contrary. They do not like to be disturbed, though, and should not be bothered in the early days. In the wild, it may sometimes happen that disturbances will cause the mother to abandon her nursery and attempt to carry the young out to a safer place. Occasionally a youngster may be lost in the process. The new nursery is usually only an emergency solution and is often cold, damp, and otherwise unsuitable, resulting in further deaths through hypothermia.

African pygmy hedgehogs are first able to roll themselves up at two weeks of age. The permanent spines appear at about one month, and the white "nest spines" fall out. At this stage they start to go out foraging with their mother and taking their first solid food. After six to eight weeks, the young can be regarded as independent and they lose interest in their mother, brothers, and sisters.

When breeding hedgehogs in captivity, the mother and litter must be disturbed as little as possible, as she too can move her youngsters and look for a new nesting site. I have known hedgehogs both in the wild and in captivity, who, like some rodents, will bite their litters to death when their stress level becomes too high.

It is possible to watch your tame hedgehog suckling her young if you are careful. Just like young puppies suckling on their mother's teats,

In the wild, littermates stay together even after they are old enough to go out foraging with their mother.

young hedgehogs knead with their feet on either side of the teat to stimulate milk production.

The juveniles: Once the young are old enough to go foraging with their mother, they soon become agile on their feet and can even climb, with further improvement each time they go out. Should one youngster lag too far behind, it lets out loud peeping noises. The mother immediately returns, followed by the rest of her litter, to seek the lost youngster. Once found, the youngster is sniffed all over and then placed back in the procession with its siblings.

This care will be given only to her own offspring. I once observed a wild mother hedgehog come across a "lost" youngster from another family and it was angrily driven off!

At about two months of age, young hedgehogs lose their milk teeth and gain a set of adult teeth. During the changeover, the youngsters constantly smack their lips and swallow, are easily frightened, and seem to be in pain. However, the process is of only short duration.

In the wild, littermates stay together for quite a long time in the nest, but as soon as they go out foraging with their mother, they start to get curious about the outside world, and each night they get further away from each other (see page 8). When they return to the nest to sleep, they get on well and lay down together in order to keep warm. Sometimes one hedgehog will push under another in order to get its back warm. When they are awake, they will play together, and with head-butting actions will practice defending themselves. Directing the forehead spines forward they will thrust them at their adversary and endeavor to make it back off. They also bite each other in these minor scuffles, but this rarely causes injury. Such practice comes in handy for driving away rivals later in life. Hedgehogs raised in captivity also show this behavior.

The Senses

Sight and Hearing: All varieties of hedgehogs are generally regarded as being short-sighted, especially during the day. If you suddenly turn on the light in the room where they are situated, they seem hardly to notice. Wild hedgehogs barely react to sudden car lights and even a strong flashlight shone directly in the hedgehog's face will cause little reaction.

Protracted bright (electric) light or bright daylight will cause hedgehogs to stay put in the undergrowth. The hedgehog cage should thus never be strongly lit. Young, or half grown hedgehogs, however, will run about the house, strong lights or not!

I have seen young wild hedgehogs of various species actually basking in direct sunlight, although this was never during the hottest part of the day. Adult hedgehogs seen sunbathing are usually sick individuals trying to get warm.

Although the data is not conclusive, various experiments have suggested that hedgehogs are color blind, seeing only in "black-and-white."

In contrast, the hedgehog's sense of hearing is outstanding. Squeaking, jingling, hissing, and similar noises cause instant reactions of fear or curiosity. They immediately set their forehead spines forward to protect their face. They never seem to get accustomed to such noises, and captive hedgehogs will continue to react however often they hear them. Normal tones are also heard, and hedgehogs will respond to the sound of a human voice. Tame hedgehogs, as I have discovered, even recognize individual voices. When I have visitors, my hedgehogs react to my voice (they will come to me on command), but will be wary if a stranger should try to speak to them.

Smell, taste, and touch: The hedgehog's olfactory sense is very well developed, and is probably its most important sense in regard to foraging. Experiments have also shown that the mother hedgehog recognizes her offspring by their scent, and that the youngsters recognize each other and their nest by the scent as well. Once you have kept hedgehogs for a while, they will come to you for food, recognizing you by your scent. Should strangers offer food, they will panic and run away rather than accept the food.

Helga Fritzsche has ascertained that hedgehogs will even recognize a dog from its scent. A dog belonging to a friend of Ms. Fritzsche was brought up with hedgehogs, who consequently had no fear of him. When a visitor came with another dog, however, the hedgehogs immediately rolled themselves up, although there was no reason for them to be scared. Fortunately, wild European hedgehogs always remain wary and never lose their instinctive caution.

The sense of smell works closely with the sense of taste, a double function that also applies to humans. Both smell and taste are chemical sensors. And so one says: "That makes my mouth water." When hedgehogs snuffle, they continually lick the air with an outstretched tongue, probably to taste the scents.

As for the sense of touch, tactile sensitivity in the digits is poor, but is very well developed in the whiskers. The long, stiff hairs along the flanks and between the spines are also very sensitive to touch. Should these be only lightly stirred and a message is sent via the nerves to the brain, the hedgehog will immediately react. The most sensitive parts of the hedgehog's body are the head (especially the top), the neck, and especially the nose and whiskers, situated just above the corners of the mouth.

Balance and Orientation

Hedgehogs are sensitive to disturbances in their balance. If one is carried about in the house, or if it is continually turned on its back, it is likely to vomit! I would therefore advise that tame African pygmy hedgehogs be handled as infrequently as possible.

When we first started to keep hedgehogs at home, we sometimes took them on an outing in a cage to a local wood. Though the trip in the car was only 15 minutes long, the hedgehogs always vomited. I would therefore recommend that hedgehogs not be carried around or taken on car outings unless it is absolutely essential.

The sense of orientation is well developed in hedgehogs. Captive animals soon get to know their "territory" very well indeed. They have an almost universal learning process: first they walk, snuffling and looking along the walls, along hedges or shrubberies (in a garden for example), along steps, and along the edges of ponds. In a very short time they know exactly where obstacles are situated, and what is the quickest route from one point to another. The territory is divided into areas with safe resting places, good foraging routes, and so on. If you allow your hedgehogs the run of the house, they will soon go their separate ways, and find their own favorite place under a seat, under the bottom shelf of a bookcase, behind the heating radiator, and so on. And each place will be defended against rivals!

Grooming, Social, and Territorial Behavior

If you have to go around with an armor of sharp spines, it would seem that you would have some difficulty in keeping clean. But hedgehogs clean themselves every day and this is often accompanied by the most incredible contortions! They shake themselves frequently, and scratch regularly, especially after waking from a nap.

Scratching is done first with the left, then with the right, rear feet. Even the head is scratched. The shaking movements arrange the spines and hairs in order after they have been disarranged during sleep. After self-anointment, the hair and spines are also rearranged by shaking.

Hedgehogs are not socially gregarious. If they don't keep out of each other's way, they can come to conflict. Captive hedgehogs, as well, are best kept in separate cages. Once I saw two sick hedgehogs in a container at a veterinarian's office. It was not long before they erected their forehead spines and began to fight. If we had not separated them immediately, it is clear there would have been injuries.

Young hedgehogs from different nests will not tolerate each other either. It can therefore be concluded that each hedgehog must have its own cage, sleeping box, and food and drink dishes. Medicines are given to each animal individually and there cannot even be a communal "sick room!" Youngsters should be given their own accommodations as soon as they are independent of their mother, not so much that I expect them to fight, but more to see if they empty their own plates! When several youngsters are together, they try to steal each other's food and this could, sooner or later, lead to trouble.

Most wild hedgehog species, including the African pygmy hedgehog, will vigorously protect their territories. Territorial defense does not always lead to serious conflict, but occasionally fierce clashes do occur. When I allowed a number of my hedgehogs the run of the garden all went well until one met another. A noisy protest usually followed, though they never came to blows.

Intelligence

Compared with humans, the hedgehog's brain is neither large nor well developed. But it does not operate purely from instinct alone. A hedgehog can learn new things and solve simple problems, such as opening a door behind which is a dish of food. If you allow your hedgehog the run of the house it will soon learn all sorts of surprising things: the difference between the kitchen door behind which may be found its food and the bedroom door where its bed may be located, for example. It will know which door leads outside into the backyard or onto the street.

You have to be careful of the street door because, of course, you will not want your pet to venture through it. If one of my hedgehogs should stand on his hind limbs and scratch on the street door, I command "No, here!" and he will get back onto all fours and look for somewhere else to go.

Hedgehogs have a good memory. Place a few tidbits down in various spots. Next time it will go first to the exact spots where you laid them last time.

My tip: The hedgehogs that I have kept knew me well and could distinguish me from other members of the household by my scent, voice, and attitude. Should a stranger have entered, the hedgehogs would always be on their guard and would not respond to any fondling or loving words. Yes, hedgehogs are much smarter than many people may believe!

Children and African pygmy hedgehogs get along well together, but it is always advisable to supervise very young children when they play with any pet.

HOW-TO:
Understand Body Language and Sounds

Hedgehogs communicate in a number of ways, but the methods most noticeable by us humans are movements of the body (body language) and sounds. Here are a few typical behaviors and the "meanings" of each:

Body Language

Rolling up: defense, distrust, fear.

Erecting the spines on the forehead: Whenever the animal is shocked, cautious, or distrusting, the spines are erected over the forehead like a visor, so that even the eyes are protected. I have ascertained that tame African pygmy hedgehogs that allow themselves to be

When distressed or wary, the hedgehog will erect the spines on its forehead. This creates a "visor" that protects the eyes and most of the face.

82

caressed over the back will erect their forehead spines "just in case" if the head or the neck under the chin is stroked. Dogs or cats who come to inspect their prickly friend will also be confronted with a prickly visor. Young, playing hedgehogs, even when still in maternal care, will erect their forehead spines over the eyes.

Erecting spines on only one part of the body: This is always done in the direction of the disturbance. It is especially prevalent in young hedgehogs.

Laying the spines flat: The spines of the head and back are laid flat against the body, a sign that the animal has no fear. Tame hedgehogs do not erect their spines when being caressed, though it will take them longer to stop erecting their head spines.

Spines that are laid flat indicate that the hedgehog is relaxed and secure. Tame animals will keep their spines against the body when they are caressed and handled by a familiar person.

Scratching at the door: This happens frequently when one has hedgehogs free in the garden. They usually stand on

The flehmen response (which is also seen in some dogs and cats) indicates intense interest on the part of the hedgehog. Actually, the animal is trying to determine whether something is interesting or dangerous.

their hind feet and scratch on the door with their forefeet to show that they want attention, or to be let in.

The flehmen response: When the hedgehog is scenting or tasting, the snout is held high, the mouth slightly opened, and the upper lip curled up (similar behavior is seen in dogs and cats). This behavior shows that the hedgehog is smelling something interesting or dangerous. In other words, it indicates a vigilant attentiveness.

Sounds

And here are a few of the many sounds hedgehogs make:

Puffing and sniffing: These are threatening sounds, made if a hedgehog is disturbed or annoyed. The sniffing sounds are clear and sharp, and the strong respiration can be compared with blowing or puffing.

Exploratory sniffing: This is similar to the foregoing but is less sharp and not as loud. You can hear this when the hedgehog is exploring a particular area (even in the house). One could regard it as a warning to colleagues and enemies. Many zoologists consider it to be connected with echolocation, so that the animal can avoid obstacles even in pitch darkness.

Coughing: The hedgehog frequently emits a sort of cough; dry, high, and hard, but short. I consider this also to be a warning to rivals. It has been heard in both wild and tame individuals, often near a food source or a feeding dish, when several animals were in the area.

Loud screaming: A hedgehog that is in danger or severe pain lets out a loud scream that can set your teeth on edge. In this connection, it is nice to report that several of my hedgehogs scream similarly if they have to wait too long for their food! While I clean the feed dishes in the kitchen, three of my animals always clamor around my ankles and have, of course, already smelled what I am doing. Once I was disturbed in my work by an important phone call, and I thought it best to place the three back in their cages. How disappointed they were, and what a noise they made!

Chirping and squeaking: These sounds are made by lively youngsters and are sounds of contentment.

Soft, quick spluttering interspersed with soft whistling: I hear this sound every time I give my hedgehogs a dish of food in their cage. One could say it is a friendly expression of thanks, with some excitement.

Continuous soft whistling: This is done by tame hedgehogs that are accustomed to

Puffing and sniffing, like the spitting sound made by cats, are threatening noises meant to induce another creature to cease and desist.

their surroundings. I only hear it when I take the hedgehog out of its cage and place it in its exercise area (either in a room or in the garden). I consider this to be a sound of contentment.

Short repeated whistling: This sound is rather piercing and loud, and is usually emitted by youngsters that have become separated from their mother.

Sounds emitted while sleeping: The European hedgehog is known to snore, but the African pygmy hedgehog is also a master at it! As well as snores (that sound, my daughter confided in me, "convivial and arousing"), you can often hear sniffing and even soft whistling. The animal is probably dreaming, much as cats and dogs do.

The Importance of Observation

If you want to understand your pet, you must watch its reactions and listen carefully to the sounds that it makes. In time, you will learn to identify most or all of the characteristic hedgehog responses described previously. You will also discover that your pet has developed its own special ways to communicate with you. Perhaps your little friend will learn to stand on its hind legs and lean its front paws against your leg when it wants attention—as one of my hedgehogs did. This special kind of interaction is one of the great joys of having a pet.

Useful Literature and Addresses

Books

Those readers who would like to know more about hedgehogs are advised to study recent books on mammals (field guides) where hedgehogs are illustrated. The following might also be helpful—especially for veterinarians:

Cosgrove, G. E. *Insectivores*.
In *Zoo and Wild Animal Medicine*,
M. E. Fowler (Ed.),
2nd edition. Philadelphia:
W. B. Saunders Co., 1986.

Gregory, M. W. *Hedgehogs*.
In *Manual of Exotic Pets*,
J. E. Cooper, M. F. Hutchinson,
O. F. Jackson, and R. J. Maurice.
Chectenham, Glocestershire, UK:
British Small Animal Veterinary
Association, 1985.

The following titles are up-to-date and intended for the general reader:

Storer, Pat. *Everything You Wanted to Know About Hedgehogs*. Columbus, Texas: County Storer Enterprises, 1991, 1994.

_____. *Hedgehogs as Pets*.
Columbus, Texas: County Storer Enterprises, 1994.

Publications

Useful newsletters that cover many aspects of hedgehog care, feeding, and housing, as well as articles on health topics are available from the following organization:

North American Hedgehog Association (NAHA)
601 Tijeras Ave. N.W., Suite 201
Albuquerque, New Mexico 87102
(505) 848-6351
(NAHA publishes the newsletter *The Hedgehog News.*)

Exotic Market Review
P.O. Box 1203
Bowie, Texas 76230
(817) 872-4130
(An excellent newsletter for more information on hedgehogs.)

Regulations Governing Trade in Endangered Species

The Convention on International Trade in Endangered Species of Wild Fauna and Flora (CITES) came into force in 1975 when ten countries ratified it. At the time of writing, more than one hundred states are party to the Convention.

The species covered by the Convention are grouped into three categories: Appendix, I, II and III.

Appendix I. Species threatened with extinction that are or may be affected by trade.

Appendix II. Species not necessarily threatened with extinction that may become so unless trade is strictly regulated to avoid utilization incompatible with their survival. Also included in this Appendix are species that are listed because of their visual similarity to other Appendix I and II species.

Appendix III. Species that any party identifies as being subject to regulation within its own jurisdiction for purposes of preventing or restricting exploitation, and which require the cooperation of other parties in the control of trade. In addition to live specimens, the Convention also applies to eggs, fur, and other parts and derivatives that can be identified as belonging to a listed species. Imports of Appendix II and III specimens are generally permitted provided that the appropriate export documentation is presented.

These are the basic principles governing imports and exports of CITES-species, however many states take further domestic measures regarding the capture, collection, import, export, sale and possession of animal or plant species including many which are not covered by CITES at all. African hedgehogs are currently listed in Appendix II; however, the appropriate authorities should be contacted for advice regarding restrictions within their jurisdiction.

Important Note:

This book deals with the keeping and care of pet hedgehogs. In handling these animals, you may be scratched or bitten. Have such injuries treated by a physician at once. It could be that some animals have a tetanus infection. This acute, often fatal infectious disease, caused by a bacillus, *Clostridium tetani*, that generally enters the body through wounds, is characterized by rigidity and spasmodic contractions of the voluntary muscles.

Some strains of salmonella are infective to humans, so always wear gloves when dealing with infected animals, and wash your hands thoroughly after every handling session. All outbreaks of the disease should be referred to your veterinarian.

When buying animals, look for signs of skin diseases caused by parasitic fungi. Skin fungi are common in our environment. The danger of skin infection increases if the hedgehog is kept in unclean surroundings or if you acquire an additional animal from a different population. The so-called "hedgehog-spots," an inflammation of the human skin (dermatitis), are caused by *Trichophyton erinacei*, and must be treated by a physician immediately.

A hepatitis-like infectious disease that can endanger humans, is leptospirosis. Luckily this bacterial infection is rather rare.

Always observe strict hygienic rules. If you have any doubt about diseases and infections, consult your physician and veterinarian at once.

Index

H. auritus collaris, 9, 71
Hibernation, 6, 8, 9, 58–59, 74
Hospital cage, 15
House training, 28

Indian hedgehog, 72
Insectivora, 6
Intelligence, 80
Intelligence tests, 6, 80
Intestinal threadworms, 50–51

Jacobson's organ, 74
Juvenile behavior, 8, 78

Limbs, 55, 62
Living quarters, 34
Long-eared hedgehog, 9, 71
Lung threadworms, 50
Lungworms, 47

Maggots, 19
Mealworms, 20, 43
Meat, 20, 43
Mites, 47
Moles, 6
Mother and offspring, 30

Nails, 23, 54
Natural enemies, 10, 66
Nest, 8
Nocturnal behavior, of hedge-
    hogs, 29
North American Hedgehog
    Association (NAHA), 11,
    12, 14, 84
Nursing babies, 44

Offering food, 20
Offspring, 15, 61, 66
Olfactory, 6, 63
Orbicularis, 73
Orientation, of hedgehogs, 79

Paraechinus, 7, 77
P. aethiopicus, 72
P. hypomelas, 72
P. micropus, 72
Parasites:
    external, 18–19, 46–47
    internal, 47, 50–51
Pets, 31
Placental mammals, 6
Pneumonia, 51
Potter, Beatrix, 4
Pregnancy, of hedgehogs, 15, 38
Puffing, 82
Purchasing, of hedgehogs, 14

Raising hedgehogs, 34
Records, 39
Reproduction, of hedgehogs,
    60, 66, 76
Rodents, 6
Rolling behavior, 59, 66, 73, 82

Scratching at door, 82
Screaming, 83
Self-anointing, 64, 65, 73
Senses, in hedgehogs:
    hearing, 6, 23, 58, 63, 78
    sight, 58, 63, 78
    smell, 6, 58, 63, 79
    touch, 58, 79

Sexual characteristics, 7
Sniffing, 82
Snoring, 83
Snout, 55
Social behavior, of hedgehogs,
    79
Somali hedgehog, 70
Sounds, 23, 82
South African hedgehog, 8, 70
Spines, 9, 55, 62, 73, 82
Spluttering, 83
Squeaking, 83
Stool sample, 21

Tameness, 31
Teeth, 6, 63
Temperature, 23, 31
Territorial behavior, of hedge-
    hogs, 79
Territory, 63, 79
Ticks, 19
Tiggy-Winkle, Mrs., 4
Toes, of hedgehogs, 6
Toys, 30
Training, 28

Understanding hedgehogs, 55

Vacations, 32–33
Veterinarian, 21
Vocalization, 64

Water, 43
Weaning babies, 38
Whistling, 83
White-bellied hedgehog, 8

Perfect for Pet Owners!

PET OWNER'S MANUALS

Over 50 illustrations per book (20 or more color photos), 72–80 pp., paperback.

AFRICAN GRAY PARROTS (3773-1)
AMAZON PARROTS (4035-X)
BANTAMS (3687-5)
BEAGLES (3829-0)
BEEKEEPING (4089-9)
BOSTON TERRIERS (1696-3)
BOXERS (4036-8)
CANARIES (4611-0)
CATS (4442-8)
CHINCHILLAS (4037-6)
CHOW-CHOWS (3952-1)
CICHLIDS (4597-1)
COCKATIELS (4610-2)
COCKER SPANIELS (1478-2)
COCKATOOS (4159-3)
COLLIES (1875-3)
CONURES (4880-6)
DACHSHUNDS (1843-5)
DALMATIANS (4605-6)
DISCUS FISH (4669-2)
DOBERMAN PINSCHERS (2999-2)
DOGS (4822-9)
DOVES (1855-9)
DWARF RABBITS (1352-2)
ENGLISH SPRINGER SPANIELS (1778-1)
FEEDING AND SHELTERING BACKYARD
   BIRDS (4252-2)
FEEDING AND SHELTERING EUROPEAN
   BIRDS (2858-9)
FERRETS (2976-3)
GERBILS (3725-1)
GERMAN SHEPHERDS (2982-8)
GOLDEN RETRIEVERS (3793-6)
GOLDFISH (2975-5)
GOULDIAN FINCHES (4523-8)
GREAT DANES (1418-9)
GUINEA PIGS (4612-9)
GUPPIES, MOLLIES, AND PLATTIES (1497-9)
HAMSTERS (4439-8)
IRISH SETTERS (4663-3)
KEESHONDEN (1560-6)
KILLIFISH (4475-4)
LABRADOR RETRIEVERS (3792-8)
LHASA APSOS (3950-5)
LIZARDS IN THE TERRARIUM (3925-4)
LONGHAIRED CATS (2803-1)
LONG-TAILED PARAKEETS (1351-4)

LORIES AND LORIKEETS (1567-3)
LOVEBIRDS (3726-X)
MACAWS (4768-0)
MICE (2921-6)
MUTTS (4126-7)
MYNAHS (3688-3)
PARAKEETS (4437-1)
PARROTS (4823-7)
PERSIAN CATS (4405-3)
PIGEONS (4044-9)
POMERANIANS (4670-6)
PONIES (2856-2)
POODLES (2812-0)
POT BELLIES AND OTHER MINIATURE PIGS
   (1356-5)
PUGS (1824-9)
RABBITS (4440-1)
RATS (4535-1)
ROTTWEILERS (4483-5)
SCHNAUZERS (3949-1)
SCOTTISH FOLD CATS (4999-3)
SHAR-PEI (4334-2)
SHEEP (4091-0)
SHETLAND SHEEPDOGS (4264-6)
SHIH TZUS (4524-6)
SIAMESE CATS (4764-8)
SIBERIAN HUSKIES (4265-4)
SMALL DOGS (1951-2)
SNAKES (2813-9)
SPANIELS (2424-9)
TROPICAL FISH (4700-1)
TURTLES (4702-8)
WEST HIGHLAND WHITE TERRIERS (1950-4)
YORKSHIRE TERRIERS (4406-1)
ZEBRA FINCHES (3497-X)

NEW PET HANDBOOKS

Detailed, illustrated profiles (40–60 color photos), 144 pp., paperback.

NEW AQUARIUM FISH HANDBOOK (3682-4)
NEW AUSTRALIAN PARAKEET
   HANDBOOK (4739-7)
NEW BIRD HANDBOOK (4157-7)
NEW CANARY HANDBOOK (4879-2)
NEW CAT HANDBOOK (2922-4)
NEW COCKATIEL HANDBOOK (4201-8)
NEW DOG HANDBOOK (2857-0)
NEW DUCK HANDBOOK (4088-0)
NEW FINCH HANDBOOK (2859-7)
NEW GOAT HANDBOOK (4090-2)

NEW PARAKEET HANDBOOK (2985-2)
NEW PARROT HANDBOOK (3729-4)
NEW RABBIT HANDBOOK (4202-6)
NEW SALTWATER AQUARIUM
   HANDBOOK (4482-7)
NEW SOFTBILL HANDBOOK (4075-9)
NEW TERRIER HANDBOOK (3951-3)

REFERENCE BOOKS

Comprehensive, lavishly illustrated references (60–300 color photos), 136–176 pp., hardcover & paperback.

AQUARIUM FISH (1350-6)
AQUARIUM FISH BREEDING (4474-6)
AQUARIUM FISH SURVIVAL MANUAL
   (5686-8)
AQUARIUM PLANTS MANUAL (1687-4)
BEFORE YOU BUY THAT PUPPY (1750-1)
BEST PET NAME BOOK EVER, THE
   (4258-1)
CARING FOR YOUR SICK CAT (1726-9)
CAT CARE MANUAL (5765-1)
CIVILIZING YOUR PUPPY (4953-5)
COMMUNICATING WITH YOUR DOG
   (4203-4)
COMPLETE BOOK OF BUDGERIGARS
   (6059-8)
COMPLETE BOOK OF CAT CARE (4613-7)
COMPLETE BOOK OF DOG CARE (4158-5)
COMPLETE BOOK OF PARROTS (5971-9)
DOG CARE MANUAL (5764-3)
FEEDING YOUR PET BIRD (1521-3)
GOLDFISH AND ORNAMENTAL CARP
   (9286-4)
GUIDE TO A WELL BEHAVED CAT
   (1476-6)
GUIDE TO HOME PET GROOMING
   (4298-0)
HEALTHY DOG, HAPPY DOG (1842-7)
HOP TO IT: A Guide to Training Your Pet Rabbit
   (4551-3)
HORSE CARE MANUAL (1133-3)
HOW TO TALK TO YOUR CAT (1749-8)
HOW TO TEACH YOUR OLD DOG
   NEW TRICKS (4544-0)
LABYRINTH FISH (5635-3)
MACAWS (9037-3)
NONVENOMOUS SNAKES (5632-9)
WATER PLANTS IN THE AQUARIUM (3926-2)

Barron's Educational Series, Inc. • 250 Wireless Blvd., Hauppauge, NY 11788
Call toll-free: 1-800-645-3476 • In Canada: Georgetown Book Warehouse
34 Armstrong Ave., Georgetown, Ont. L7G 4R9 • Call toll-free: 1-800-247-7160
ISBN prefix: 0-8120 • Order from your favorite book or pet store

R 6/94